CW00859481

FACING THE STAR-GATE

Exploring the dimension of faith.

R H Brassington

Facing the Star-gate

Published by R H Brassington & Printed by CreateSpace, an Amazon.com Company, Seattle USA – 2014

ISBN-13: 978-1500425968
ISBN-10: 1500425966

This book is dedicated to all those people with whom I have had lively conversations about science, religion and the existence of God—

I hope it provides food for thought.

R H Brassington.

About the author.

Rex Henry Brassington BTh.Cert.Ed.

Moving from a career in electrical engineering Rex went on to study Religious Education and Science through the University of Nottingham's faculty for Education, Matlock, Derbyshire, during the early 70's. Further academic studies were pursued with both the Church of England dept. for Christian Education, and Mallon de Theological College W. Yorks. He has also been a keen member of the British Society for the Turin Shroud since the mid 198o's. Prior to retirement Rex taught RE in schools in South Yorkshire and Derbyshire.

Today both the author and his wife are members of *Lifehouse Church*, Chesterfield – Part of the Assemblies of God network world-wide. He also maintains an active contact with the local Holy Trinity Anglican church, and the Church Army.

During recent years Rex has experienced a growing passion for Creation research - the overwhelming evidence for Intelligent Design. This is something which is becoming more and more acceptable amongst scientists and biblical scholars, in spite of frequent opposition from militant atheism. His passion for Creation and biblical anthropology naturally brings focus on Genesis, and with it the importance of our understanding of the ancient world as recorded in the Bible. It is with this aim in mind that the book is written.

When not involved in church activity the author enjoys spending time in France and has a love for its language and culture. But his favourite pleasure is his family.

Contents

Acknowledgements

It was during the early part of the millennium that through much discussion with Christian bookshop manager Mick, that I was able to discover the existence of what today amounts to a vast resource on Creation research which helped inspire this book to be written. I often felt that his arguments for God's *six day creation* were so overwhelming that it was almost like the irritating grit in an oyster, which although was uncomfortable at the time, had the potential to produce "treasure" - so thanks to Mick Lowry-Fields. I also owe much gratitude to all who have devotedly applied their academic and literary skills in proof reading, professional criticism and advice: Sister Jill Hancock, Peter Bower, Brenda Pegge, Peter Topliss, Rev. John Bellfield, Garry Morson, Graham Allen, Fiona Woodhouse and Pastor Jim McGlade. Not forgetting prayerful support from church members, plus special thanks to the present-day family who allowed me to write about their great grandfather. Last but not least a big thank-you to my wife for her patience and hours spent in reading through many manuscript chapters during the last two and a half years of writing this book.

Foreword

Over the last four decades I have devoured hundreds of books but *FACING THE STAR-GATE* is unlike any other book that I have read. How Rex weaves his central message around a man who lived in the last century is quite unique and refreshing.

Writer and historian, Hendrik van Loon began his *History of the World* with these words "We live under the shadow of a gigantic question mark. Who are we? Where do we come from? Where are we bound? Slowly, but with persistent courage, we have been pushing this question mark further and further towards the distant line, beyond the horizon, where we hope to find our answer. We have not gone very far'.

If you are looking for purpose and meaning then *FACING THE STAR- GATE* is a must read for you. It is a pull no punches and right to the point read that will point you in the right direction. This book is also a valuable tool for every Christian who would desire to equip themselves so that they can confidently give the reason for the hope that they have. I commend it to you.

Jim McGlade,
Former Senior Pastor of Zion Church (now Lifehouse Church) Chesterfield

Preface

Facing *the Star-gate* is a book about all those thoughts and feelings we sometimes get when we stare at the heavens on a crisp clear night. It's about science and religion. Although at first this might sound heavy, it is not intended to be written with the need for any great depth of scientific or theological knowledge. It is written by a "man in the street", for a "man or woman in the street" who may be desperately trying to make sense of Christianity in today's fast changing and confusing world - or just simply to grab faith and get on with it! Now and again I'll come across somebody expressing their confusion over science and religion documentaries on TV which have left them very much in the dark when it comes to biblical matters. And I believe many people have been spiritually damaged by what can even be distortions of what is essentially the absolute truth - which brings me to the aim of the book. It presents a contemporary illustration of the Bible's story, whilst at the same time addressing some awkward counter issues - which often create more questions than answers - and then hopefully cast positive light on what I call "the dimension of faith". Although there is a necessity to examine some profound issues, I trust the book is also easy and pleasant to read. For this reason whenever a subject area might seem to be getting too academic I try to lighten the tone with the occasional change of voice or style. And, contrary to good penmanship, may even resort to the odd spot of rambling.

Every time I visit Chesterfield market my imagination often focuses on the town pump in the centre of the stalls. It was here in 1777 where John Wesley preached his profound gospel message to hundreds of people in the open air. I've often wondered what would happen if anyone were to try that today. They would probably last about five minutes before someone told them that what they were doing was illegal and must cease immediately. So much for our progress in free speech! And so it is that Chesterfield has some significance for me when it comes to powerful preachers of days gone by.

There is also another story and another preacher, who did not hit fame like the great Wesley but who, if anything, was more of an unsung hero as evangelists go, and probably today hardly anyone has ever heard of him. A Chesterfield man, family man, coal miner, and member of the Salvation Army; William Sanderson helped set-up one of the first soup kitchens in Chesterfield during the early 1900's. He was, to say the least, a humble Christian soul whose personal miracle inspired him with what we might call "one good sermon", which was to become his life's mission. As far as we know he never preached from the town pump, nor for that matter drew any vast crowds like John Wesley, but did receive occasional invites from other churches and institutions in order to tell his story.

Readers might ask: "what has an old time preacher got to do with science and religion, especially in our modern technological age?" Well the simple answer might be: "why should our times be any different to any other; has human nature changed?" No! And neither has the preacher. The preacher has not always come over as Mr. PC Nice-guy, in fact sometimes he's been pretty unpopular. The good ones have usually stirred us all up and made us think – and made us think about real life issues like why are we here etc! As for myself I neither have the freedom nor the inclination to copy any of the preachers of the past in their skillful transmission of the spoken word, but I can, in a similar driving spirit, create my own *town pump* by using the written word, and achieve the same purpose. One might also ask: "for whom is this book written?" To which I would reply that it's written for anyone with ears to hear—or if you like; who chooses to stand in front of "the town pump", that it might encourage the faithful and challenge the doubters.

Rex H Brassington

"How then shall they call on him in whom they have not believed? and how shall they believe in him of whom they have not heard? and how shall they hear without a preacher?"
Romans ch10:14 . King James Bible

"Town Pump"- Chesterfield market place

Introduction

This is a book about science and religion, or more accurately, science and the Bible. The Bible is unique in that it has within it the means of its own defence and does not need to rely on external "proof" for its existence, which is why it has survived so long. Over the centuries it has inspired and enthused men and women from all walks of life, who have demonstrated time and time again that its ideas work. However, many of science's technological advances also work and have benefitted life as a whole. This is what is known as *operational* science which deals with proven repeatable experiments on which we can soundly base some of our present day technical wonders. However when dealing with our past, particularly our ancient past, science has to follow a more forensic style, searching for and interpreting evidence; for this reason it is often referred to as *historical* science. Sometimes science might appear to clash with the Bible, but if science is interested in the pursuance of truth then there should be no conflict, as both have a common aim in discovering our ultimate destiny. The book is also about faith, which I believe is a tremendous source of inner strength, enabling us to have purpose, hope and the means to survive. What this book is *not* about is anti-science. On the contrary it hopes to show an embracing of science and how the right scientific worldview can be a tool which might empower the faithful in witness and also inspire many others to pursue further research.

Facing the Star-gate

I chose the idea of a *star-gate* for a title because such concepts often dream up thoughts of mystery and intrigue that we often find in science fiction. Although in recent years, imaginations seem to have shifted away slightly from ET and alien abductions to more of a focus on secret codes, which could shatter our sacred idols or even unlock some secret of the universe. Our nostalgic romanticizing of the past rarely fails to grab the imagination and will never be too far away from gazing at the stars. Ironically though, science fiction is so popular these days that we'd sooner believe in some embroidered fabrication of what DaVinci's latest secret is than the reality of Christ's Resurrection, which has had a profound effect on our planet for 2000 years.

If I were to attempt to grab the reader's attention from the outset, I might try the popular approach and start by having someone discover some secret manuscript hidden in a recently unearthed chamber in the Valley of the Kings, or wherever, which would solve the world's economic problems or scupper the very foundation of life as we know it.

Such popular film or book starters usually succeed in grabbing our imagination in the mythical hope that; "Hey! I wonder if one day they might even find one of those star-gate things, or something, that can transport us to another world ?" Conversations deepen, especially late at night or in frenzied chat with some good mates, sitting next to a traditional log fire and sipping a pint or two in the pub snug. It's from here that I also wish to inspire a little "Dan Brown" enthusiasm myself, but by claiming my own *real* "manuscript discovery".

In contrast to the attractive world of science fiction however, a vivid imagination is not required. In fact much of the ideas in the book represent stark reality and are not meant to be entertaining. Hopefully you will see the real *star-gate* that was not discovered in the Nubian desert but rather in your own back yard so to speak.

I aim to focus on the dramatic story of a man called William Sanderson who lived in Chesterfield, England during the early part of the last century. The story is so mind-blowing that it has often provoked intrigue, discussion and even argument when told. When I first heard it told by someone close enough to have known the man, it had a profound effect and consequent trigger for my own faith, which helped set me on a new path. But this was not without difficulties, and further on, the book represents some of my own questions and doubts I had during those early years. We must appreciate that when some people come to faith it can be so dramatic that there is rarely any need for many questions afterwards. As for most however, it might be less dramatic and more gradual. Because they now see the world through a new pair of glasses, some of the old questions, which still irritate, need to be examined under this new light – that is, a new belief or worldview requires a new understanding – this was my own experience. It's an exciting path which can take the new believer just about anywhere, even to realizing that "everyone has within them a book"; so this is it – my testimony, observation and plain talk.

William Sanderson's story is another testimony. Not just to the power of a living faith, but to a life which is a benchmark for us all. I believe the account to be true and his message (his "one good sermon") to be relevant. Over the years I've seen how stories like this have been a useful catalyst for teasing out some of those discussion questions that I have heard many times before over the years in the classroom, workplace or the pub. It is one of those stories that quickly shifts the tone of superficial small-talk into deeper levels of more philosophical discussion around what we might call "first order questions" such as: "why are we here and where are we going?" I hope I might be excused for my occasional northern colloquial style, as many of the points raised are based on gleanings from banter and debate, both flippant and serious, which is often found amongst "real folk."

So let's imagine that group of "good mates" in the pub snug on a Friday night, or some similar stage setting, mulling over dreary conversations about the week's typical drudge. As philosophical comments slide deeper into "what's it all about?" banter, followed by long pauses which indicate that conversation material could run out at any moment, someone throws in a nice little spark – or rather a story about a man who was raised from the dead! This not only resurrects a dying conversation but also livens up the next half hour or so. Now, I've noticed that whenever this kind of conversation emerges and the tone swings, it nearly always seems to follow the same pattern. Stories about raising the dead and miracles are a bit like the splash of a stone in a pond which radiates out into ripples or subjects. What starts with the weird, Divine or religious at the centre can quite often end up in the galaxies as offshoots, covering ideas from Charles Darwin to Stephen Hawking as well as the Bible.

And so it is with this book, I've used William Sanderson's story as that splashing stone hoping it might provide useful surf for all the other questions – or ripples.

For the *Message* in chapter nine I have used a more dramatized style of writing in an attempt to capture a *church and sermon* atmosphere, whilst at the same time trying to keep the facts accurate. I have left the *message* near to the end of the book because I think that the reader might be better prepared by airing some major viewpoints discussed in the earlier chapters.

Let me make it plain from the outset that I think atheism is a bit of a non-starter. Isaac Newton once said of it; "It is so senseless and odious to mankind that it never had many professors". If you claim that God doesn't exist then how can you disbelieve in something that's not there, for a start? Even a good gambling man would put his money on there being a hereafter; at least he'd be able to collect his winnings if he were right! Perhaps being more agnostic might be a safer bet, and anyway you don't get many atheists in life-rafts, or as Harry Secombe once said "in the trenches". When the chips are down we usually need a good mate even if it's a Divine one. Atheism sometimes might seem a useful idea especially when it suits a cosy, affluent lifestyle, but for someone who needs faith, comfort and hope during times of grief, pain or sheer hopelessness, atheism has some serious limitations.

For me the journey of discovery did begin in my "own back yard" or in this case, Chesterfield. In the second chapter we take the clock back, not two or three thousand years but about a century ago, to about 1909. The site an old tin mission, the manuscript, an old preacher's Bible. Hiding between the pages of the Bible; a sheet of paper with a hand written message, and a story that might even make Da Vinci raise an eyebrow.

~

Chapter 1
What is this life - this journey ?

What is this life if, full of care,
We have no time to stand and stare.
No time to stand beneath the boughs
And stare as long as sheep or cows.
No time to see, when woods we pass,
Where squirrels hide their nuts in grass.
No time to see, in broad daylight,
Streams full of stars, like skies at night.
No time to turn at Beauty's glance,
And watch her feet, how they can dance.
No time to wait till her mouth can
Enrich that smile her eyes began.
A poor life this if, full of care,
We have no time to stand and stare. --------- *William Henry Davies.*

For most of us who live life in the fast lane and the so-called "real world" we rarely have much time to even consider such realities as important -- least of all "sheep and cows". That is of course until faced with the reality of our own mortality. Primarily, the idea of the *star-gate* represents that final journey that we all must make when we leave our comfortable existence on this planet of ours. And facing it, or rather being aware of its tremendous implications, can and I believe should have, a direct bearing on how we spend what little time we have here and now, whilst we yet breathe.

Of course that *matey banter* around the pub table is often a veneer concealing a serious interest. Some of the ideas raised in the next few passages are simple examples of the thoughts generated by that *stone in the pond,* illustrated in the introduction, which provide fuel to reach further into topics which are as much about science as faith :-

I so often see so many people live life on earth as if they're going to be here forever, when in actual fact we all know they're not! Building vast empires, amassing piles of wealth and possessions, better homes, bigger cars, better swimming pools, only to find that man is like grass, here today and gone tomorrow, and the kids swoop in on the cash! Even the educational system ingrains into our kids the need for high achievement, so that you can get a good job for good money, for a big house, flash car and more! OK education is good and Heaven forbid, let's not neglect the importance of combating ignorance, after all our kids need everything they can get to arm themselves against some of the deadly experiences that life on earth might throw at them. But what education and what values? Sadly today's fast high pressure world seems very much akin to a "survival of the fittest" mentality where top dogs with the loudest bark seem to get the most attention, where *Coronation Street* and *East-enders* is true life and *Songs of Praise* makes nice make-believe telly for the dwindling few.

On the other hand I see a growing hedonistic culture which says that because you're not going to live forever, it's better to "eat, drink and be merry for tomorrow we die". In other words "you don't know when y' times up an' yer a long time dead!" It seems to be quite a gloomy trend which seems to see little point or purpose in life, which is only some Darwinian accident anyway, and because the end justifies the means, it's best to "get what you can while you can." After all we're just the result of a few chanced molecules which happened to be spinning around in some sort of primeval slime a very long time ago!

Sadly both view-points are wide of the mark.

I don't know if you have ever noticed that the older you get the more funerals you seem to go to. And when you do go you seem to get nearer the front every time. This is probably life's little joke, as if to say; "one day it'll be you up there". And oh! How it's softened by "a good send-off" when what's really important is a good arrival! And funerals really do punctuate life! We've all gotta go sometime, so surely anyone who can get round that one is worth listening to!

Some years ago I can remember a student picking up a "Good News Bible" and asking what, or where, was the good news bit in it. Its words and sentences seemed to be so daunting, in spite of the modern translation, that in the end he decided simply to ask. Whether the following answer to his question was the one he expected or not I suppose I'll never know, but he did seem somewhat thoughtfully content as he went away. Basically the Good News, or "gospel" as it is in Greek, is that simple fact that the Bible's main point is Jesus. God, who in human form visited planet earth 2000 years ago, entered our world and cared enough to put His life on the line for our sake just to bring us the key to the universe and complete a mission that we could not complete ourselves. The "Good News" is simply a message which revealed a key-pattern for mankind that if embraced guarantees us safe passage and indeed safe arrival when our time comes. ----"Hmm!" Was the student's reply, "I never saw it that way, I suppose that is good news".

Jesus was the Master of the art of living and the message He brought, the gospel, was the most explosive and challenging message of all time. It not only cost Him His life to deliver it but since then although the message took the world by storm, man has for some reason or other done his best to try to destroy, discredit or even counterfeit it. Such is the magnanimity of this gospel that when we come into contact with it, as we do from time to time, it never fails to challenge us one way or another. This gospel whether received as attractive, irritating or downright repulsive is a star-gate which stands before us and will not go away. On one hand the illustration of the *star-gate* is that which we will all pass through into eternity whether we like it or not, on the other it represents the message of Jesus which we stand before and ponder.

Pastor W E Sanderson

The message of Jesus was re-iterated in a very powerful way during the life and death of Pastor William Edward Sanderson during the early part of the last century. As far as modern illustrative gimmicks such as star-gates were concerned they just simply weren't around, but indeed reality was. William's *star-gate* was certainly real, as one who was, beyond all reasonable doubt, literally raised from the dead, brought back to life to tell the story, and even brought back a message, later to become that "one good sermon" as mentioned in the preface. So profound was his message that I believe it is the best advice ever, and gives due authenticity to the story. Not only that but the message is a wake-up call for lots of those "churchy types" who like the mouse in the biscuit barrel who thinks he's a biscuit, also think that because they go to church they're ok, when in actual fact they might not be.

So without further delay let's now go straight into the story, after which we might need to reflect over a cup of tea before reading the rest of the book.

Conclusion

The *star-gate* tells us that:

Life is everything precious and time on earth is relatively short.

We journey towards an eternal destiny whatever our world-view.

The gospel of Jesus gives us great hope of a great future and therefore must command our attention.

Chapter 2 .

The Story

"Yea, though I walk through the valley of the shadow of death, I will fear no evil; For You are with me; Your rod and Your staff, they comfort me."- Psalm 23:4

William Edward Sanderson was born in 1878 and died in 1910 ---- and then again for the second time in 1954. He lived for most of his early life during the harsh Victorian times when one appreciated a hard day's work for a hard day's pay! It was a time of what we might call an axis of change which was soon to come upon England and in turn the rest of the world; things would never be the same again. The motor car was just finding its wheels; electricity and the telephone were unaffordable novelties. The Wright brothers were still doing "bunny hops" trying to get off the ground and radio was nothing more than a scientist's dream. Needless to say the advent of the First World War was on the horizon. It was also during a time of social and spiritual change. The pioneer William Booth, founder of the Salvation Army was zealously fighting the social evils in the East end of London, whilst at the same time early Pentecostal revivalists and reformers such as Smith Wigglesworth were re-discovering the power of that old gospel message. **1**

W E Sanderson's life was indeed extraordinary and even more extraordinary was his death. Having had the pleasure of knowing his granddaughter for many years prior to her "great re-union", I was able to obtain from her and other reliable sources, information about this amazing story. I thank her, and indeed her family, many of whom are alive today, for granting me the privilege of sharing his testimony.

As an ordinary working class family man who held strongly to what we term today as good old fashioned Christian values, William was the salt of the earth. As the sole bread winner of a large family the need to be in regular employment was paramount. William was a coal miner and knew what hard work was. When you were off sick in those days - that was it! You didn't get paid. There was no social security to guarantee an income and life was tough. All you had was the Parish money to help keep body and soul together, and if that wasn't enough to keep the family together, there was always the dreaded Workhouse, and that was just about the last straw. When the chips were down, and quite often they were, faith was about all you had left. It was this *faith* which was to become one of the greatest testimonies of all time in William Sanderson's life.

It was during the year 1908 that William began to suffer from tuberculosis or what was called consumption in those days. Cures were few and far between and often victims of this terrible scourge would be later admitted in to what was called a sanatorium - a kind of specialist hospital situated where the air was cleaner than the usual smog of the town or city. Sufferers who could afford it were sent to the seaside. For instance, Scarborough once had a clinic for consumption suffers. However, this path was not to be taken in William's case.

As a coal miner- and a tough and proud breed as they were - with family responsibility, William was to battle on with his daily work down the mine in the hope that the problem would perhaps be healed by some Divine hand, or just go away.

As the illness gradually tightened its grip during the winter of 1909 William became weaker and found himself at home more than he was at work.

The following account contains exact details from an original manuscript as William E Sanderson wrote them shortly after his life-changing experience:

The story.

"In January, 1909 I began to get much worse; my work, when I could get to it ,was a real burden to me; in fact I could not work. I began to cough very heavily and to spit blood. During February I became still worse and my strength was failing fast. On the night of February 22nd,1909 I went to my work. My wife did not want me to go for I was so weak that I staggered through the doorway like a drunken man and got to work with great difficulty, but I was useless for it seemed as if all my strength left me."

Coal mining, particularly on the coal face was a pretty hard and demanding task and working in such unpleasant conditions would often take its toll no matter how fit one might be; needless to say nightshifts were of no help. Teamwork and comradeship were of the essence if one were to survive some of the many hazardous incidents which often occurred. William often referred to his workmates not as mates but as "brothers" in his original scripted story. The "family", indeed some were even blood relatives made it their duty to look out for each other.

"Between one o'clock and half-past in the morning my brother and mate went to get their "snap" *(lunch pack)* they wanted me to try to eat some but I did not want any, being too ill to eat. Just at that time we were going through a very dangerous piece of work as the lower part of the "stall" *(coal face)* had fallen in and we were anxious to get through, it was the main air way for the district, and we had almost made a way through. While my brother and his mate were in the gate eating their snap I just remember picking up a coal ringer *(a large iron bar used for leverage)* to try and force a road through but remember no more".

William had dropped unconscious at the coal face and when his mates came back to the stall they found him stretched out on the floor. His brother claims they "lifted him up, shook him and tried to get him to speak" but to no avail. Wasting no time they then carried him to the gate-end, a distance of about four yards, when, to their horror about four tons of roof fell in on the very place where William would have been lying about a minute earlier. It doesn't need much imagination to realise that that would have been the end of the story – but for the intervention of that Divine hand which became the hero of the tale!

Help was immediately sent for from the next gate (a gate being a tunnel connecting a coal face). The situation now ran into full speed. The pit deputy ordered a stretcher team to carry him to the pit bottom, then to the surface via the shaft to the lamp cabin where a doctor could be

telephoned. After his examination the doctor suggested he be sent home and later visited him for further examination. He told William and his family that his chances of regaining consciousness were poor and they gave "very little hope of his recovery".
They certainly were a tough breed in those days, for William was not to be finished so easily. That mysterious Divine hand was intent on playing a different game, for indeed William did pull through, yet not without major problems:

"Well I continued bed-fast for about two months and gradually got a little better so that I managed to get up, then got about a little, though the cough and blood spitting were making a terrible rack of me, for it was increasing fast. I was losing flesh rapidly till I was almost a shadow and began to stoop and could only get about with the aid of a stick, for I was bent like an old man of great age and was almost double.
My memory began to fail me and I could not remember anything and became almost childish, for I would pick up toys and bits of string or pot or anything and used to have a pocket full and play with them like a little child, in fact the neighbours began to think I should have to be taken away."

Being appreciative of small mercies and true to his faith, William Sanderson decided to take it upon himself to go to church at the Salvation Army hall. After all it was a Sunday morning – and that's what you did! The Salvation Army hall was a small missionary building, often nicknamed in early revivalist pioneer days as the "tin mission". Sometimes the meetings would be held in a hired room during the early days of the movement. The mission itself possibly existed beyond the Lower Pavement end of Chesterfield towards Markham Road, probably not too far away from the later established

Salvation Army building which has also now disappeared to make way for development.
To make the journey from his home on the other side of town on a Sunday morning, a distance of about a mile, would for most be a pleasant walk after a hearty breakfast, but not for William who was in such a shocking condition. Such was the depth of this man's faith and obedience to His Lord and Saviour that he was greatly rewarded and blessed. During the time of prayer he received renewed strength and the regaining of his senses; "—for in three days I was as sound in mind as I am today".
Although it seems that an experience of the unexplained had occurred William was far from being "out of the woods" and actually seemed to be getting worse. His body was still in a shocking state as he himself described:

"Then It seemed so strange that I started having fits very bad, it was really a mystery where strength came from for it took seven or eight men to hold me during these fits, yet at other times I could scarcely hold up. My cough increased and I commenced to vomit blood as much as a pint at once, and it was a mystery where all the blood came from. At this time I had been attended by seven doctors and none of them could do any benefit. They held out no hope and said it was impossible for me to survive. I had been to Scarborough hospital but they could not do me any good and ordered me to a sanatorium, but the doctors at home said I could not be accepted as I vomited too much blood. I was like that poor woman in Luke chapter 8:43, for my wife had spent all she had and sold all possible, still I became worse and had to be put back to bed. The fits came on more and more; my shoulder and legs became so sore that I could scarcely abide for the friends had to put all their weight on me to hold me down. I never had to be left alone, night or day. No one knows but God and myself the pain and agony I endured. I became so feeble I could not hold a teaspoon and had to be fed with a feeding bottle. Then something started in my head for it burned like a furnace and for a fortnight I was covered with ice bags; none of the doctors could ease my suffering. During that time a man named brother William Lunn, a real man of God, earnestly prayed to God to heal me, and he did not become tired of praying but held on to God although it seemed useless for I became worse; the doctors said that my right lung had become completely gone and my left lung was in rags. My wife was almost heart-broken and my little ones looked at me as I stood by my bedside and their mother used to fold her arms around them to comfort them, and loud sobs and deep sighs did she give as she looked on my death stricken face as she thought every moment that her little ones would be left fatherless, that the one she loved could be taken from her side.

My father brothers and sisters stood broken hearted by my bed expecting to see the one they love pass from time to eternity."

This was on a Sunday morning in January, 1910. The Salvation Army held an open air meeting not far away; they being sent for came to the room. And they looked on me fighting for my last breath they stood around with their hands linked and sang softly and sweetly:

> We shall walk through the valley of the shadow of death,
> We shall walk through the valley in peace:
> For Jesus Himself shall be our leader
> As we walk through the valley in peace.

Of course I knew nothing of this for I was too far gone. The bandsman looked upon me, expecting it to be their last look at me alive. They then went outside my window to play my favourite hymn. Brother Hall moistened my lips with cold water, and whilst they played my favourite hymn "Wonderful words of Life" I passed away to be with Jesus.

The bandsmen went very sorrowfully. You can imagine the feelings of my wife and little ones, and my father, mother, brothers and sisters. It was a sad time for them. The blinds are drawn, notices sent to my relations and their blinds also drawn: the people tried to comfort my family and then dispersed, tears streaming from

their eyes. Word reached Brother Lunn as he was concluding the children's service at the Mission, so he closed at once.
Then he cried to God saying "Well Lord, it was you who led me to pray for him".

What followed defies all sense of logic and human perceived wisdom. I know there'll be those of us who will on one hand scoff and just pass it off as; "well we've heard all this sort of thing before an' well it's probably some sort of chemicals in the brain an' all that which triggers when you pass-out, y' know like some of the science stuff we've seen on the telly". Of course we're all very good at "telly-wisdom" which makes everything authoritative. It's just a pity some of us don't take the time to do our own research instead of being spoon fed all the time by the "experts" who probably got most of their ideas from some other "spoon" in the first place. I sometimes wonder why it is in this modern scientific world that we can readily accept the idea of multi-dimensional universes, time travel, little green men, Harry Potter, and yet struggle with a simple idea of the reality of an after-death experience. On the other hand there will of course be those who will have no problem with such accounts. After all there are countless numbers of similar world-wide cases, and even if more than half were proved to be bogus there will always be the ones left that leave us with the only alternative; that sometimes the simplest explanation is often the right one!
I don't think it's too difficult to grasp that if someone were to have such an experience as William E Sanderson they would never be the same again. And one might even excuse them for being religious about it – if not profoundly so! Religion is only an outer expression of an

inner experience culminating in a belief. For instance have you ever had the thrill of a gift you've always wanted and then wanted to shout and tell everyone about it? Or experienced your favourite team score a winning goal at a cup final? Ecstasy is nothing on that one! Arms in the air, shout for joy –

"---deep in my heart I do believe that we shall overcome-om-oome -!"

"-- United ! United! United forever!

You can even almost hear a faint amen at the end. And the talk about it in the pub after is electric!
Now if that's not religion what is?
So perhaps at the side of this it's not quite so easy to knock the man who's just been given his life back plus an encounter with that Great Team Manager Himself ! If he uses some religious jargon like" Hallelujah" or "Praise the Lord", well, wouldn't you?
Continuing from the original manuscript written in William's own words, this is what happened:-

"During the time that I had passed away, I was talking to Jesus. Oh, how I would have liked to have stayed with Him! But my will could not be His will: His will is the best.
I received a great many instructions from Him which I must be faithful to carry out as some are very secret. He told me to send for the two brothers, and gave me a message to give them, and that they must be obedient to carry it out, then He would perfectly heal me. He gave me other instructions which are between me and my Precious Lord Jesus, sent me to carry out all that He had commanded me, breathed breath into me and my dead body became alive again.

You will understand what happened when the blinds had to be drawn up again, news had to be sent to my relations and their

blinds to be drawn up. Soon people gathered together in my room, my wife, children father and mother, and many other friends gazing with great amazement at me, in fact they were afraid.
I asked for the two brothers so that I could give them the instructions from Jesus. They were sent for, for they had gone home with sorrowful hearts and never expecting to see me alive again. When they returned and entered my room, they came with fear and trembling to my bedside with pale faces, and as I delivered unto them privately that which Jesus had told me, they followed the instructions, and the Lord Jesus gave them the assurance that He would heal me, and as you will read further on, He was true to His promise.
I was not raised up straight away, I was still compelled to keep to my bed for I was not yet healed. Time went on till one day as I lay in bed the very same One I had been with when I passed away spoke to me. Yes I knew the voice so well – it was Jesus – and these were the words He said: "Thou shalt rise on the 15th day of February." I thought February had gone, for I remember something of the commencement of it, but it had seemed so long I really thought that other months had gone by for I was many a day in an unconscious state, so I asked the woman who was nursing me what date and day it was; she said she did not know but she would enquire. The answer was that it was the 14th day of February, so I said, "Well, I am going to get up tomorrow for Jesus says that I am going to rise on the 15th." She smiled and others smiled too.
God kept me conscious throughout the whole of that day, and I believe I had more visitors than ever. I told them all I intended getting up the next day. They seemed amazed for I was too weak even to raise my arms, which had to be raised for me. They tried to soothe me and pass it off, but I would keep telling them that I was going to get up. But one dear sister who came to see me – one that really knew the Lord - said to my wife: "As far as we can see it is impossible for him to get up, if he should ask for his clothes you must give them to him".

Facing the Star-gate

Night came and it was a terrible night of real pain and agony, a real fight with the enemy, but still the words of Jesus stuck to my memory and I knew that He spoke the truth.

Morning came – the 15th day of February had arrived and I was worse than ever. Right throughout that day I lay with my eyes closed and never asked for a drink of water. They say that all day I seemed to be gasping for my last breath, and that the doctor, when he examined me, said I could not last the day out and probably should not regain consciousness, and that they must watch me closely or I should be gone and they not know. They trod softly about the bedroom so as not to disturb me, and everybody thought that instead of getting up I should be going up yonder to be with Jesus. The people gathered to see if what I told them on the day before would be right. At ten minutes to five in the evening that sweet voice of Jesus called me to arise. I opened my eyes, strength came into me and I arose. Some that were in the room fainted. I sat on the bed-side pleading for my clothes.

Praise the Lord for great things He has done,
Hallelujah !

My brother Fisher gave me my clothes with a trembling hand and wanted to help me to dress but I was able to dress myself. I wanted them to let me go downstairs but my friends did not wish to let me go unless someone assisted me for they were afraid of me falling headlong; but I would not let them help me for I knew that the Lord Jesus would not let me fall, so they let me go downstairs on condition that someone went down before me, to this I consented on their promising that they would not touch me. I landed downstairs alright and the armchair was padded for me to sit in, but I did not sit down just then. I asked for some water – cleanliness being next to Godliness – and when it was brought I stripped and washed myself as well as any man could wash himself.

When I had washed, the Lord Jesus spoke to me again and said: "Trust and thou be faithful", and as I looked round I saw on the shelf a pen, ink and paper; these I took down and wrote the message and by the Grace of God, I mean to trust Him and be faithful. I drew the armchair to the table – the chair was well padded for I was only a mere shadow – and asked for my tea. I am sure I sat for not less than twenty minutes before I could get any tea for they were all afraid to let me have any. At last I got some and made a good meal.

> Praise the Lord for He is worthy to be praised;
> He is still Jehovah, the enough God. Hallelujah!

Word was sent to Brother Lunn and he was in pit clothes when he came. I shall never forget him for when he came in he raised up his arms and said: "Praise the Lord! Don't be alarmed; I know all about it; the Lord has revealed it all to me while I was at work." My wife and others wished me to return to bed but I would not go. My father came and he almost sank to the floor when he saw me in the chair downstairs. He tried to persuade me to go back to bed. The house was filled with people who had come to see if what I had told them the day before had come true, and much to their arrangement they saw me sat in the chair. About 7 O'clock I began to get weary, so I consented to go to bed. There were soon plenty of hands ready to help me upstairs, but I would have no assistance for I was able to go alone; but my father said he must assist me for he feared I should fall. As I walked past him to the foot of the stairs I said "You may if you can catch me," and as he rose to take hold of me I was at the top of the stairs; it seemed as if God lifted me there. Several followed upstairs. I seized Brother Lunn and Brother Fisher (each weighed over 12 stones), and threw them in the air. We went down before the Lord and gave thanks to Him for His wonderful work. Oh, hallelujah! There is nothing too hard for the Lord.

Glory to Jesus, for He is so precious to me. Then I undressed and went to bed, and had a night's good rest – The best I had had for some months. I got up daily but could only get about by the aid of a stick for I was bent almost double. On the 5th of April, about

Facing the Star-gate

10 -30 a.m. as I knelt by the bed-side talking to my dear Lord, a voice spake to me, yes I knew the voice so sweet to me, it was JESUS ! And these are the words He said to me: "Arise and put away thy stick, for thou art now made whole."

I did not arise from my knees just then but kept praying. I felt a warm glow of something I had never felt before, and again the Lord Jesus spake the same words to me. And I arose and was completely straight. I went downstairs at such a rush whereas before I had to come down gently in a sitting position from one step to another. My wife was knelt down cleaning the fireplace, making ready for me to come down so she could leave me comfortable whilst she fetched the Parish money – for we had to be kept by the Parish as we had nothing else. She turned in amazement, her face went pale as death, and I said to her "where's my stick?" She had lifted the fire-guard as she cleaned, my stick used to hang on the corner of the guard beside the armchair in which I used to sit. The stick had fallen to the floor, so I said to my wife: "Put it away on the shelf, as I don't want it any more; God has completely healed me." She could not get up to put it away, so I put it away, so I put it away and have never wanted it since.

Praise the Lord for He's just the same.

I was a new man, strength had come into every part of my body, I marched about filled with praise unto God. Yes it was enough to make me praise Him for His wonderful healing power. The Holy Spirit began to teach me the word of God and I knew that I must be obedient to Him all the way, so on the 11th of May, I was buried with him in baptism, (Romans 6 – 4) Brother Lunn took me to Bethesda mission Chesterfield, and the Rev. T. Smith baptised me. Hallelujah! it was glorious to follow the example of my Precious Lord Jesus .

On the night of the 15th August a few of us had gathered together and, as we were waiting upon the Lord, the Holy Spirit fell upon me as it did at the beginning. I shall never forget that, talk about praising Jesus! The Holy Spirit was praising and glorifying Jesus through me. Since then, God has wonderfully used me for His Glory in leading a great number of souls to the Precious Lord Jesus and also many wonderful cases of healing.

"Jesus is the same, he faileth not. Hallelujah!"

I pray that this testimony will inspire the heart of every dear reader to trust the Lord for all things for He is the God of the Body as well as the Soul, yes, He is the Great Physician. I have now been examined by the best doctors we have and they cannot find any trace of consumption. They say my heart is perfectly sound, my lungs stronger than a natural man's lungs.

" Hallelujah! To God be the Glory,
Great things He hath done."

I am just in the hands of the Lord, to follow out the purpose for which He has healed me.
For this purpose, that Jesus might be glorified, I am open to take special meetings, missions etc., that precious souls might be brought to the Lamb of God, who died in our stead and bought us with the price of His own precious blood."

I remain,
Yours in Jesus,

PASTOR W.E. SANDERSON.

It was pastor Sanderson's unique experience which had in it a far more universal relevance than just the sensationalism of a miracle. I am referring of course to the encounter William had with Jesus and the important message he had to deliver to the church. It is this message, explained in chapter nine, that I consider so important that the miracle of coming back from the dead is secondary to something which, although written over a century ago, is as relevant as ever it was. Furthermore because of its relevance and the strong parallel with the teachings of Jesus as recorded in the gospels, I believe William's penned script to be genuine. "Jesus *being* the same Yesterday, today and forever". (Heb.13:8).

Conclusion

- William Sanderson's experience was real and his illness, death and miraculous recovery was witnessed by several people of whom relatives are alive today.

- The experience had such a profound effect on his life, and although the Chesterfield landscape has since changed several times, the spirit of his message lives on.

- Further authenticity of his experience is borne out by the content of his message to be delivered to the church which strongly reflects Jesus' teaching in His Sermon on the Mount.

Reference and notes.

Julian Wilson. *Wigglesworth the complete story,* (Milton Keynes:Authentic-Publishing,2002)
A fascinating account of Smith Wigglesworth's life and how he demonstrated the miracle working power of the Holy Spirit. Wigglesworth was one of the pioneers of the Pentecostal movement which over the years has made a vital contribution to the charismatic church world-wide. (1859- 1947)

Derby Daily Telegraph – Aug 22nd 1931:-

FULL GOSPEL MISSION
SONS OF TEMPERANCE HALL.
Walbrook Road, Derby.
SECOND VISIT OF
PASTOR W. SANDERSON,
of Chesterfield, who will preach
SATURDAY, Aug. 22, 7.30. p.m., and
SUNDAY, Aug. 23, 10.45 a.m. & 6.30 p.m.
Bring your sick to be prayed with.
Hearty Welcome to all. 200p

Derby Daily Telegraph – Jan 31st 1914:-

REVIVAL. REVIVAL.

MISSION HALL, GEORGE ST., DERBY

(OFF FRIAR GATE).

16 DAYS' MISSION

Will be held in the above place from

SATURDAY, JAN. 31, to SUNDAY, Feb. 15,

To be commenced by

MR. WILLIAM SANDERSON,

of Chesterfield, who will tell how God raised him from Death unto Life, and healed him of that terrible disease, Consumption. He was given up by the doctors. They said it was impossible for him to live, but God raised and healed him through prayer. He has now been tested by doctors, and they cannot find any trace of disease. All the glory is to the Lord.

Don't miss this. All are welcome. All seats free, Hymn Books provided.

TIMES OF MEETINGS:

SUNDAYS—11 a.m., 3.30, and 6.30 p.m.

Week Nights 8 p.m.

Chapter 3.

Pause For Thought.

Now you either believe that or you don't. It's an amazing story and the message is quite a package. Of course depending on the reader will determine the type of reaction you get. You see there's a bit of a risk involved here in that it might make us feel slightly uncomfortable if we have to start believing in God when we don't want to. Spooky stories are ok for the majority because they either bolster an existing belief, excite the imagination or just give us something to laugh and poke fun at, that's probably why they make good movies. But if we're faced with ideas like Jesus and God then it's a matter of the "packaging" affecting the "cringe factor". In other words wrap it up with a load of pious churchy language and you just might find yourself geared up and relevant to meet the needs of the 1950's ! But if it connects with the now and speaks 3rd millennium culture then you might find you have less "deaf ears". Also the word "God" is not always understood. For some the idea of God is nothing more than a very large bigot and failed control-freak in the sky, who lives in creepy looking stone churches (places obviously to avoid) and is only interested in starting wars, creating dodgy priests and spoiling our fun. Well if that's God then I don't believe in him either!

But I do believe in an absolute creative intelligent force which permeates the entire universe and beyond, who not only consists of pure love but who is also interested in little me! Now if I'm being offered a chance to get to know this guy then I'm interested! Also when I read pastor Sanderson's "message" I feel that its words contain "iron", and connect very well with both the state of the church and the nation in these modern times.

Thank God I'm an atheist

There appears to be a stir going on at the moment, much of which seems to be attributed to a rather vocal gentleman by the name of Richard Dawkins. Retired professor, who also claims to be an atheist, Dawkins seems to be pouring vast amounts of time effort and cash into trying to abolish religion. He's probably got more chance of knitting fog if the truth's known. I mean we're talking about three quarters of the world's population or so, that is if we include Jews, Muslims, Hindus and Sikhs as well as Christians. His "New Atheist" movement (although it's nothing more than an old atheist one tarted -up) seems to champion its "crusade" at just about every opportunity. Armed with well-rehearsed rhetoric and cash (Dawkins himself of course is not exactly on the bread-line) both he and his cronies wheedle their way onto the "telly", write books, open up atheist camps and have even started an "atheist church" – all apparently in the frantic attempt to, not just abolish religion but God as well! The ironic result of all this is that in their evangelistic and organised attempts to get rid of religion they've actually started one!

If a so called atheist church has regular meetings (usually on a Sunday) to preach about God, admittedly in a negative sense, has dogma and doctrine on what to believe and what not to believe, spends time in moments of silence, sings relevant songs and thereby creates its own ritual, it must be about as close to a religion as you can get! I'm amazed that someone can go to great lengths to rant on about something that they believe is not there. I mean I don't think that many of us believe in fairies at the bottom of the garden or flying pigs for that matter but we don't make a fuss about it. So why someone wants to preach a belief about non- belief just stuns me. And it gets even sillier when Dawkins and his ilk spend big cash to have posted in big letters on a London bus: "*There's probably no God. Now stop worrying and enjoy your life*". It can only imply that the word "probably" means he doubts his faith. Furthermore if there is a God then, does that mean both he and his like have to worry? I think he's so far down the road now it's nigh impossible to change — I think he's terrified!

It's a strange psychology that when most people argue the toss against God they're sometimes secretly wanting answers. I've recognised this trait in people who have a way of using you to test out their own fears and doubts. Quite often they'll go away and think about it. I've even spotted the odd one using such pro-God arguments against other challengers as if giving it all a re-test. There are also others who think that if they rant on vehemently enough gaining popularity on the way they can somehow persuade God not to exist, a sort of crisis denial of the problem hoping it will go away. Or shrugging the shoulders and playing the "only being honest card", you know as if it's God's fault for not paying them a personal visit. Maybe Dawkins is in this league - maybe one day he'll get his visit!

The idea of believing in God, for some people, may be a fear of not knowing rather than knowing. It's also possibly a fear of church or of getting roped in to regular commitment or even some weird cult. I can understand this. When I became a Christian, for example, I didn't want to join a church straight away but was quite happy to go along every now and then to the occasional service or fellowship. For me Christianity was, and still is, not so much about religion but relationship. My relationship with God, and with people, is an on-going discovery which is what it's all about. All in all being a Christian is a spiritual path rather than a religion. You don't have to go to church to be a Christian - true, but it helps if you do. I like a good sing, I like to hear a good sermon and I like to chat with like-minded people. When you become a Christian you are the "Church," i.e. part of the universal community, the invisible church or church without walls if you like. The idea of church is to enable like-minded believers to relate with and support one-another, it can even take place on the internet. Church is also a community which hopefully seeks to leave the world in a better condition than when it found it. I find it invaluable. It's not only a place to express worship, but also to extend that worship in practical service to others. Having said that of course, part of the church's job description is to accept all comers, warts an' all; "Come to Jesus as you are" goes the preacher's welcome. That's the church's responsibility; the Christian's is to allow God to do His bit by shaping us from the inside out and making us the best that we can be. As I said Christians are on a spiritual path and although others might see it as "pie in the sky when you die" it's also "steak on your plate whilst you wait". In other words although it might at first seem all heavenly minded and out of touch with reality, its earthly use is meant to enrich daily living. We're all at different stages on the way, there should be no competition no racism, ageism or prejudice etc. There are however those who struggle with problems of life and encounter difficulties as well as the super saints who just seem to sail through. After all a church is a place for sinners, not a museum for saints and maybe the only institution which exists for non-members. It is in this context that the church community comes into its own, each supporting one another and working out his or her salvation!

So when all is said, purveyors of atheism are "up-a-gum-tree" on this one because frankly they're trying as much as they can to destroy the very fabric which helped make this country and others great. History shows that most of the pioneers of science and social reform were often people who were inspired by a positive religious conviction. To dismantle this kind of inherited structure would plunge us into totalitarianism on par with communist USSR of the past or some other atheistic regime that the world has witnessed. I can only surmise that people like Dawkins who once held a professional position in one of the top universities in the country must now have become a source of embarrassment to some of his more level headed associates.

No wonder the Bible says: "The fool has said in his heart there is no God". (Ps.14:1).

A faith for the nation

William Sanderson's miracle story is one thing, his lifestyle is another. Simple soul, simple family values; Christian lifestyle. Imagine if every family in Britain were to embrace Christian values today then most of the country's problems would be solved over-night. Values like honesty, morality, altruism and mutual respect would get an extra boost. Honesty in business would be restored, addictions and crime would decline and families would be strong and in turn so would be the nation. However, that would take a miracle – but why not? Christian revival has happened before and it can happen again. The mistake is to think that we have outgrown God and can do the job better.

The Christian lifestyle works now and has worked well for the past 2000 years and although it seems to be less popular when the living is easy and abundant, attitudes can quickly change when things start to go wrong. For example whenever there's a national crisis look how many people turn up at church.

We only seem to want God when it suits. To get us out of a sticky mess or to give somebody a "good send-off" at a funeral. Or even to simply pin the blame on.

Anne Graham Lotz (Billy Graham's daughter) made a remarkably apt comment on just this very thing.

She was interviewed on the Early Show (USA) after the fierce devastation left by Hurricane Katrina in the southern parts of USA in 2005. Anne Graham Lotz gave an extremely profound and insightful response:

Pause for thought

Jane Clayson: 'How could God let something like this happen?'

Anne Graham Lotz: 'I believe God is deeply saddened by this, just as we are, but for years we've been telling God to get out of our schools, to get out of our government and to get out of our lives. And being the gentleman He is, I believe He has calmly backed out. How can we expect God to give us His blessing and His protection if we demand He leave us alone?'

God seems to hold proof of His existence in fine balance. One can neither prove nor disprove His existence, so it seems. Yet people today seem to *want* proof. Show us a miracle! But why? Would that really convince? If you want to see tricks and illusions find an illusionist. If it's entertainment you want find an entertainer. God is not in the showmanship business, miracles usually happen when life is at the cutting edge and backs are flat against the wall. I think in William Sanderson's day values were different, faith was important and for such as him, God was as much a part of the fabric of every-day life as food, clothing and shelter. We live in a society that is self-sufficient now, comfortable, and without much thought for the need for God. If we want healing we see the medics. If we want cover we get insurance. If we want fun we get fun, hobbies, holidays or just the pub. Live now pay later might be ok for now but sooner or later someone has to pick up the tab.

Conclusion

So here we have the story and the witness to God's powerful existence. I believe through my own research into an account which took place over a century ago that the facts are genuine and William Sanderson was raised from the dead, miraculously healed, and he did meet a real and living Jesus. It's an amazing story which even gained a spot of fame at the time and witnessed by many who came to hear William preach, tell his story and even pray for the sick. In just about every way his story is no different from the stories in the New Testament where followers of Jesus went about preaching the gospel and healing the sick. They did it because they too had met the Risen Lord and were fired with the passion to tell others. The difference is the story of William Sanderson gradually became forgotten within a few years whereas the account of Christ's Resurrection and the impact it had is told today worldwide. William Sanderson was only a man and servant. Jesus is King and Saviour. So I don't think we need *proof* of God's existence because I think the facts speak for themselves and would be pretty obvious to most people.

It's now at this point in the book where the emphasis shifts from the *splashing stone* in the pond to some of the ripples created. To some of the many questions and points that might be raised by either the lads chatting round the pub table or just about anyone, anywhere, for that matter.

Pause for thought

So having now taken a little time to gather a few thoughts, let's begin the quest. Let's begin with the most profound book on earth – the Bible; starting at page one and beginning with the earliest record of Creation – Genesis!

Chapter 4

In the Beginning - Time

"In the beginning God created the heavens and the earth".—Genesis chapter 1,verse 1.

Harry was a keen cyclist, always dashing up and down Main Street, zipping from central station to local village paper shop eager to get the early, and for him the earliest, newspapers on the newsagent's counter before any of the other lads in the neighbourhood got theirs. His bike, pride and joy, was his steed as the dashing express rider raced with Wells Fargo zeal in an attempt to beat yesterday's stopwatch. With aspirations of one day becoming a champion cyclist, time was always the one to beat. Time was also relative to pace, and indeed never a constant. I suppose for Harry, like any other young lad of his day, dashing around and filling life to the brim, words like "boredom" and "slow" hardly found a space in his vocabulary. That is of course until the day he cut one of those time saving corners in the road and came off!

For Harry this was no new experience, for such as it was worth, scrapes and close calls were always to be trophies and battle scars earned as evidence of good training - scars worn with pride amongst his rivals.
The thing that mystified him however was that every time he took to the air and gracefully glided over the handlebars leaving the bike to shoot off in a different direction to himself, it seemed to take an awful long time before he finally hit the deck! Whether or not the floating slow motion effect transmitted any thoughts of impatience or boredom, it certainly gave him time to negotiate the landing.

Harry's experience is common to many and although we laugh at the funny side to all this I think there's quite a serious link. I don't know about you, but the number of times I've fallen off things and witnessed that "weird time lag", seems to be something which happens to lots of other people as well. And of course there are other examples. It's no secret that the older you get the more time seems to whizz! When I was young time seemed to be time. Minutes seemed like hours and days like weeks, especially during school-time's drudge. On the other hand the holidays were over in a flash! Of course looking back on all this it only seems about five minutes ago. So what's all this about I ask?
Take sleep for example. I can nod off for a few seconds to wake up realizing I've just lost an hour of waking life! And if I'm painting a wall the clock can almost stop! Heaven forbid if I have to watch the paint dry.

So all in all, it seems that because of our human perception, certain circumstances can give us an illusion that time is not constant but relative to an observer. Of course in the world of research *illusions* of time are a far call from the rationality needed for it to be proper science. Albert Einstein however, had an amusing way of explaining "relativity", which might hint that the human factor is important after all:

"When you are courting a nice girl an hour seems like a second. When you sit on a red-hot cinder a second seems like an hour. That's relativity". **1**

Weird, strange and bizarre as it might be the phenomenon of time is reality and whether or not we use a clock to measure it, time will exist anyway. Something which might seem a useful marker to the business of time, is what scientists call *entropy* (the 2nd law of thermodynamics), which basically tells us that as time passes things change or wear out. And for us that is a pretty good "clock"!

Physicist Brian Cox describes it like this:

"The Arrow of Time dictates that as each moment passes, things change, and once these changes have happened, they are never undone. ———We all age as the years pass by — people are born, they live, and they die". **2**

If we were to ask "When did time begin?" it might beg the question as to "What time was it when the clock (a device for measuring time) started ticking?" which in turn would need reference to another measuring device (clock?) for determining when the clock started. Science tells us that the universe began about 13.7 billion years ago and it all happened with a big bang! Was there anything before that? We don't know.

The fact that we (science, philosophy or otherwise) can conceptualise a "before" might suggest that the beginning of the universe was not necessarily the beginning of time, and that time was sometime before that. If so, any "before time" might be better described as eternity.

Time and Genesis

We are taught throughout the entire Bible that God is the Creator of all things - the "Alpha and Omega the beginning and the end" (Rev.22:13). This means if God created all things then He must have created time. We know that God is eternal, therefore He stands outside time which, I think, puts him in a good position to create it. It's a bit like saying if I want to create a motor car I have to begin from outside the thing first and foremost, after which I can start to work from within it as it takes shape. Plans and even drawings can exist within the mind of their creator right down to their fine detail. Eventual speed, handling and expected length of service can be accurately predicted even before time and motion is ever put to work on the vehicle. And all this can be held within the timeless mind of the creator. This I believe is key to how we may understand Genesis chapter one in the Bible. God didn't need to take billions of years to create the universe because all the planning preparation and design had already been done billions of years ago, if you want to put a time value on it. All He had to do was to release the mechanism or as it says in Genesis, speak the word.

I often think it's rather like one of those two-second tents we see nowadays. My grandchildren love them.

Here's a thing that probably has had years of tent design and technology poured into it for it to be suddenly released into the full grown perfect tent at the pull of a string. Rapid creation! Better still, and nearer the point, what about a seed like an acorn? All that intricacy of engineering brilliance released by self-assembly into a mighty oak!

Creation in six days

Genesis chapter one - Overview:-

Day 1 - Light is created separating day from night.

Day 2 - The "firmament", "heavens" or atmosphere is created.

Day 3 -The waters are gathered together and dry land is formed. Plants, vegetation, and trees are created. Each one is designed to reproduce only seeds after its own 'kind' or type.

Day 4 - The sun, the moon and stars are created.

Day 5 - Sea creatures and birds of the air are created and created to reproduce with and after their own 'kind'.

Day 6 - All land dwelling animals are created. Finally .."God creates man in His own image" from the dust of the ground. He commands man to multiply and to rule over the rest of creation and have responsibility for it.

Day 7- Continuing in chapter two, Genesis states that God now seals his Creation by emphasising that it was ... "very good". Thus the 7th day God rested from his creative action.

It is quite plain as most theologians will tell you, that the writer of Genesis chapters 1 & 2 intended the reader to take it as literal history. The process of the release of

In the Beginning - Time

God's Genesis project follows a logical and yet simple pattern. There's no need for complicated theoretical and pseudo-scientific guesswork, God in His genius has made profoundly simple that which would normally be impossible for man to understand. Although the Bible may not appear to be a scientific book, when it does touch on science it is surprisingly accurate.

The opening verse states emphatically that it is God and He supreme who created the heavens and the earth (the universe). Immediately the Creator is a person; 'He'. Not it, or some intelligent impersonal force, but 'He'! Creator, Sustainer, Designer and Prime Mover of everything in existence. Genesis next states that the first thing to appear was planet earth. Earth was covered with water as God's Spirit moved over its surface. Then God spoke: "Let there be light and there was light ...so the evening and the morning were the first day".

A common misunderstanding is to assume that the "light" in day one was sunlight. Genesis does not mention the creation of the sun until day four. Genesis states that the earth was created first, which although contrary to *big bang* science does follow a particular logic. The clue, I believe, to all this is in the understanding of the term "light"! We pick up this particular use of the word several times later in the Bible. For instance in John chapter 1 Jesus is seen as the Light of the world that lightens every man. At the resurrection the witnesses experienced angelic light. Further on the concept of Divine light comes as a heart experience to the believer at the point of conversion. Saul (later Paul) of Tarsus was struck by a blinding light resulting in his conversion. Even "wise-men" followed a cosmic light at Christ's birth. And light is always seen as creative, intelligent, purposeful and good, and that which overcomes darkness, ignorance and gloom. So to make the point, the light at Creation was supernatural by all accounts. Creative, intelligent energy source, containing all the information and DNA for the universe, by such an act contained time also.

God, "Who covers *Himself* with light as with a garment: who stretches out the heavens like a curtain" Ps.104:2.

Light, time and physics

In Dr John Hartnett's book *Starlight Time and the New Physics* he explains how Einstein's theory of relativity shows a distinct relationship between light and time. He goes on to describe a recently popularised hypothesis called the "inflation theory", which suggests that as the universe expanded milliseconds after the Cosmic Big Bang everything was being created including time itself. He mentions that some scientists have further claimed that constant laws of physics may not have been the same at creation, particularly in respect to the speed of light which "was much greater in the past and possibly up to a speed of 600 billion times the present value" **3**.

In other words as the universe was "inflating" or "stretching" its molecular fabric at a phenomenal velocity, light (which normally travels at 186,000 miles/sec.) was also enjoying the ride - rather like an Olympic runner running in a 100 mph train in the same direction making the total speed (time/distance) much greater.

Hartnett also explains that during the last century Edwin Hubble's *observations of galaxy redshifts indicated to him that we are at the centre of a spherically symmetrical distribution of galaxies.* He later rejected his own theory claiming the idea *was too philosophical and made the Milky Way too special.*[4] What might be seen as an old pre-Copernican idea of the Earth being the centre however could well be re-emerging under a growing number of creation scientists and as a result directly influencing the understanding of Genesis 1. For example, if God, clothed in light, stretched out the universe from a given starting point within a vast ocean of blank space, one could conclude that this same location in space was also the starting point of his mind-full energy. As God's cosmic materialisation of fabric came from this energy, earth appeared as the *first* in a long sequence of events. The spiritual was becoming physical. To a hypothetical observer it may have simply appeared to have come from nowhere or just nothing, and one can possibly understand that as far as science is concerned that would be the conclusion, although somewhat limited in its understanding. There are of course further biblical parallels which give support to the idea of sudden appearance. Take the sudden appearance, or *manifestation* of angels, for example. There are countless examples of this both in the Bible and throughout human experience down the centuries. Jesus himself appeared suddenly to his disciples after his resurrection, and is reported to have appeared to more than 500 people at one time according to 1 Corinthians 15:6. Acts of God that are outside the realm of time and space as we know it allow ideas like *time dilation,* or even something appearing in no time at all, to become more comfortable and easier to take on board. This being the case it seems quite respectable to assume that as the cosmic clock was registering billions of years in the universe, the effect of *time dilation* was showing days on earth and therefore the reason why ... *the focus of Genesis history is on earth clocks and not cosmic clocks.* **5**

As God was applying His light to earth in Genesis 1:1-2; He was also applying time as well as information (Divine DNA), gradually handing over planet earth from the supernatural *first cause* to the natural *first effect* as it materialised into being. By the time day 4 appears, the natural running and eco balance is set, leaving two final stages of 2 x 24 hours to complete the six days. It is during the beginning of day 5 where Genesis might identify with what evolutionists call the "Cambrian explosion" otherwise known as the "Big Bang of Biology" where the waters began to "teem with living creatures", as Genesis so elegantly puts it.

So how old is the earth?

The scientific methods used for establishing the age of the earth's fabric are pretty much taken for granted by most of us. Often we hear scientists nonchalantly roll off copious millions and billions of years proudly presenting how "we now know" the age of certain fossils because "we now know" the well-established age of the rocks they were found in. And this is all very much taken for granted because we were taught this from an early age and so there's no reason to doubt. Or is there?

Dr A J Monty White, former head of *Answers in Genesis-UK*, states:

"Although they (evolutionists) confidently inform us that such and such a rock is so many millions of years old we have seen that such dates are meaningless." **6**

He previously describes in the same chapter how large discrepancies of millions of years have often been erroneously mis-calculated as a result of some of the so called sophisticated "scientific" methods of dating. Not only that but he shows that the dating methods, often cited as proof of the earth being millions of years old, can also be used to show that the earth is *thousands of years and therefore young.*

Dr Monty White is not alone in this field. There are growing numbers of highly qualified creation scientists who ascribe to the same worldview. The readily available information is found on numerous creation websites plus many well- written books. There is even a dedicated research organization called RATE (Radioisotopes and the Age of the Earth) which has been set up solely for investigating this field of science. Unfortunately this vital information does not get the correct media attention it deserves. And it would be a fair comment indeed to say that there are some convincing scientific counter arguments against those of a young earth persuasion, even from scientists who also claim to be religious.

But the hanging question for me, which seems to cut a simple path through the lot, is this: If during creation, the fabric of the earth was interwoven with the creation of time itself, how can anyone living thereafter possibly date rocks and subsequently the age of the earth?! They must be trying to measure a timeless entity. Therefore there's little wonder that scientific dating methods of such a time/mass substance get so confused. It is a bit like asking how much water is in the cup whilst you're still pouring it from the kettle. If the earth has time built into it, what time? Earth time? Cosmic time? Where do we put the clock?

Time and Evolution

What needs to be recognized here is that the whole theory of evolution is totally dependent upon the accurate calculation of the earth being millions of years old, in order that the gradual development of life can happen. Without this deep time factor, gradual changes from *microbes to man* cannot happen in evolutionary terms. The idea of the evolutionary process is that it relies on millions of bio-chemical random chanced sequences acting together within a few billion years of extremely "good luck" in order to accidentally arrive at *you* and *me*. What is often referred to as "goo to you via the zoo!" Meaning that as life gradually emerged from some kind of primeval "soup" it clawed its way up through the animal kingdom to eventually become human. So if there exists serious doubt amongst scientist about the dating methods used to measure the age of the earth and the cosmos, why is evolution taught as "fact" with so much zeal, when at best it can only stand as a hypothesis? Furthermore when we realize that the cornerstone of evolutionary science is the location of fossils within certain rock layers the following statement inspires little faith in such methods:

"Rocks are dated by their fossils and the fossils are dated by their supposed evolution, which, in turn, is proved by the dates of the rocks in which the fossils are found." This is what's known as circular reasoning. Dr Monty White. **7**

Yet this powerful dogma which is taught throughout is fragile from its very core and one might ask; "whatever is it that keeps it propped up?" Because *If evolution were a building it would probably collapse*! **8**

Why I believe this is important

History has shown how Christianity has contributed richly towards the moral fibre and social welfare of Britain over the centuries, and has provided an excellent reference point for many a leader and statesman. In the past the Bible has been a leading light that has served the civilized world very well. It not only provided good moral teaching but gave reason and purpose for our existence. And to top it all it inspired millions with faith and hope. This is known simply as the gospel, meaning "good news" and we learn about it by reading the Bible. Nothing could be simpler than that, yet there are those who would complicate it, oppose it, corrupt it and even spend millions trying to undermine it. So if we're constantly being brainwashed through education and the media that we're nothing more than a cosmic accident with no purpose whatsoever, except our own survival, then is it such a surprise when things go so terribly wrong?

Dr Bill Cooper, who has done extensive research into the authenticity of Genesis, suggests that some of this opposition had originated in 19th century Germany:

It "had grown out of the so-called Rationalist Movement of the 18th century, sometimes laughingly called the Enlightenment, and the ambitious goal that it set itself, the destruction of the Bible, was to consume vast sums of money over many years, (a consumption that is still going on today).

He goes on to say how this has influenced thousands of scholars in hundreds of colleges and universities world-wide, not to mention publications and media. Dr Cooper mentions that:

"Never in all history has any human enterprise attracted so much over such a long period of time in the way of financial investment, talent and sheer devotion -------- And all this just to ridicule the Bible". **9**

Furthermore Dr Cooper goes on to say how in his experience no other book has ever received so much criticism. Yet in spite of all opposition "this school of thought is further from its goal today than it has ever been". The Bible stands today as the dearest treasure to millions despite what the critics might say.

The reason for all this is pretty obvious to me. Firstly God exists, secondly the Bible is true and thirdly when we read it we discover it has a powerful adversary, often referred to as the destroyer, but more commonly, the devil.

Such an entity hates God, hates His creation including the human race, and hates the Bible. So with this in mind is there any wonder the Bible gets a slating!

St Paul said: "For we do not wrestle against flesh and blood, but against principalities, against powers, against the rulers of the darkness of this age, against spiritual hosts of wickedness in the heavenly places"(.Eph.6:12)

In addition to all this, the Darwinian need for long earth time has further forced biblical scholars to compromise on Genesis, creating sufficient scepticism amongst ordinary folk that many who have been fooled into believing Genesis a myth have gone on to question and doubt the rest of the Bible. Having said all that, the Bible stands firm; its amazing resilience has shown time and time again that sooner or later its critics fall short. Not only that but it needs no propping up with science or archaeology and can stand on its "own two feet". The earth has the appearance of a certain age because discovered scientific facts have been interpreted that way. This is what is known as a world-view which is shaped by pre-conceived ideas of the observer. If a world-view preconceives long ages then the Darwinian picture will be expected to fit and this of course is equally true for that of the young earth creationist. It is the same evidence only the interpretation or world-view is different. Within our modern Western world-views of things we seem to have grown away from a simple faith in believing in miracles. It is as if we've grown out of this "childishness" and now need some reason or explanation for what was at one time the un-explained. Yet for some who claim to believe in nothing, often find themselves believing in just about anything, no matter how crazy or un-supported by any sound evidence it may be. The simple understanding of Genesis 1 as briefly outlined seems a straightforward interpretation using the time factor as the key. Not only that but as Alex Williams once claimed in a foreword to Dr John Hartnett:

"The idea that God created the universe in six days just a few thousand years ago is now not only intellectually respectable, it is a far better explanation for what we observe than its competitors". **10**

Conclusion

When Jesus healed the leper his new skin was only a few seconds old but would have had the appearance of that of a healthy grown man. When He turned water into wine in seconds the wine had the appearance of age, as it was the best tasting. When He fed the five thousand with an instant miraculous abundance of bread and fish the food had the appearance of perhaps a few hours old, yet with freshness good for eating. So if Jesus, God's son could do that then why couldn't God create the universe in six days, even if to us it has the appearance of great age ?

The gospel of Jesus has worked well during the past 2000 years. Showing itself to be a source of spiritual and moral strength, it has also provided a source of integrity for society as a whole. A message that provides faith, hope and love, peace, vision and family values, cannot be ignored, yet evidence in the world today seems to indicate that ignorance is the case.

As already stated the past has shown that the great social moral and spiritual reformers have been successful because of their unshakeable Christian faith and conviction, but this has only come about as a result of their total belief in the authenticity of the Bible, and that includes Genesis. Liberalists and half-hearted preachers never seem to have had the same results.

Dr A C McIntosh, professor of Thermodynamics at the University of Leeds claims:

"When revival has come, the men God used in revival have always been men with an overwhelming conviction that all scripture is the inspired and infallible Word of God". And that "this has been the hallmark of evangelical faith". **11**

If our nation is to be rescued from its moral and social decline, then it starts with Genesis.

Notes and references

1 http://www.brainyquote.com/quotes/authors/a/albert_einstein. Nov.2013

2 "Brian Cox and the arrow of time" http://www.brainpickings.org/index.php/2012/03/29/brian-cox-arrow-of-time

3. Dr John Hartnett. "Starlight Time and the New Physics" (Powder Springs: Creation Book Publishers.2007), P22

4. Ibid. P74.

5 Ibid. P20.

6 Dr Monty White. "What about origins" (Leominster: Day One publications. 2010) P106.

7 Ibid..

8 Dr William Dempski. "The Delusion of Evolution" (Nottingham: New Life publishing.2010) 4th edition. P6.

9 Bill Cooper. "The Authenticity of the Book of Genesis" (Portsmouth: Creation Science Movement Publishers. 2013) P14.

10 Alex Williams; Former consultant (and Australian representative) to the United Nations'International Atomic Energy Agency, and co-author of *Dismantling the Big Bang: God's Universe Rediscovered.* Foreword cited in Hartnett, "Starlight Time and the New Physics".

11 Dr Andy McIntosh, professor of Thermodynamics. Leeds University."Genesis for today" (Day One publications. 2001). P108

In the Beginning - Time

Chapter 5.

Eden 4000 BC - the walled garden.

***The "Temptation seal"* 2200 *BC. British museum* 1**

Let's take a journey back in time to about 6000 years ago, to a place somewhere deep in what was probably then a lush fertile valley within the walled protection of the Zagros mountains. Within what is part of the Ararat range of present day Iraq and Iran, we might possibly have witnessed a richly adorned tribe of warrior type land guardians called Kerubim. Dressed as ferocious winged guardians of the eastern gateway into Eden, performing ritual dance on the high places and borders surrounding a one-time paradise, these dedicated defenders held a dim memory of an ancient Biblical story. An ancient record of how angels or cherubim originally guarded the way to the Tree of Life in the Genesis account of the Garden of Eden.

Even today the town of Kerubad derived from the "settlement of Kheru", is an ancient link with the past.

Eden 4000 BC - the walled garden

Here, within the walled eco-system, the greatest and first civilization on earth began, to which is linked today every tribe and nation on earth. Egyptologist David Rohl calls this the Neolithic Revolution:

"It is now recognized that this fundamental development first came into being in the high valleys of the Zagros mountains – in the area we now identify as Eden. In effect the Biblical Adam of Eden marks the change from prehistoric hunter and warrior to spiritual man, with knowledge and technological skills. And it is knowledge which is the foundation of civilization". **2**

For centuries the exact location of Eden has been as much sought after as the Holy Grail.

Eden today

The Canadian *'National Post'* of 11th January 2001 made a claim that the Garden of Eden had been located. Michael Sanders is director of expeditions for the Mysteries of the Bible Research Foundation, in Irvine, California. After a careful study of satellite photographs taken by the National Aeronautics and Space Administration, placed the Garden of Eden some-where in eastern Turkey near the upper reaches of the rivers Tigris and Euphrates.

In this region, Sanders identified four rivers and linked them with the rivers described in Genesis.

These are the Murat River (a major headstream of the Euphrates), the Tigris, the Euphrates, and the north fork of the Euphrates. This, he says: "proves that the Bible's description of the Garden of Eden is completely and literally accurate." 3

What are we to think of such claims? Many Christians would be encouraged by this report. Should we embrace this claim wholeheartedly? It seems to support the Bible. But the fact remains that "Eden" may be elsewhere. For example some have claimed that the Garden of Eden was situated at the head of the Persian Gulf, where the Tigris and Euphrates Rivers run into the sea. 4 The site is now under water, which could even make us think about the lost city of Atlantis. Egyptologist David Rohl would however place Eden closer to the Caspian Sea under the Ararat range in a valley area known as Tabriz between Armenia and Kurdistan. 5 Ancient Egyptian merchants under the rule of queen Hatshepsut often referred to an *Eden like* area, rich in resources, such as gold and ivory, and abundant with natural beauty and wildlife, called the Land of Punt, located somewhere on the southern coast of the Red Sea. This latter location would of course appeal to the theorists that life began in Africa and headed out through the Great East African rift valley, which opens out towards the Red Sea. However Francesca Stavrakopoulou (a known atheist and biblical critic) located Eden either on the border of Iraq & Iran or in Jerusalem itself ! 6 She went on to say, "it must have been man made anyway wherever it was", which is probably what you would expect from an atheist. But giving her comment a fair hearing it's probably a useful hint towards the truth, not in the sense that it was man made but rather man replicated. The one thing that all these theories are overlooking is the *global flood* which devastated the planet, re-shaped the landforms and river courses, and left little trace of a once occupied garden by the first of mankind. The new post-flood population would have contained their memories and traditions of the old story of Eden's paradise etc. and would probably try to re-locate it or at least re-create and replicate it as near to their imagination as possible. The desire for "Eden" is in all of us, think of the number of places in the world named after it. Even the famous hanging gardens of Babylon – part of the Assyrian city of Nineveh, and what about your own back garden replica? A similar parallel happened when settlers from Europe originally migrated to North America and Australia. For example, the coal-mining city of Newcastle in Australia was named after the coal-mining city in England with the same name, and there is also a Liverpool in Australia named after the English city. North America also has English place names such as London, Oxford and Cambridge. The settlers applied familiar names to many new places in their new world. It is perfectly understandable that some rivers in the post-Flood world, like the Tigris and Euphrates, got their names from rivers that existed in the pre-Flood world but had subsequently changed their course or even disappeared altogether. And so echoes of Eden's paradise in the heart and stories of post-flood man, might also suggest that ancient civilisations, because they had stronger and more recent ties to their ancestral roots, were most likely to have had a pretty good idea where to start looking.

The Great Flood

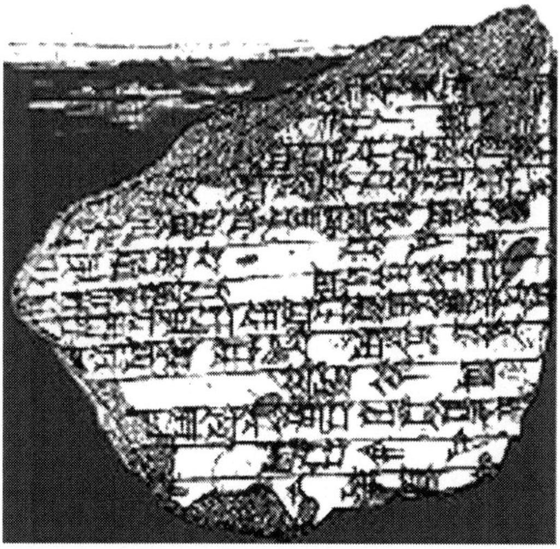

Sumarian Flood tablet 2100BC. Pennsylvania University.

About 4-5000 years ago Planet earth witnessed a global catastrophe never to be seen on such a gigantic scale since. The discovered tablet (left) is probably one of the earliest written records. **7** Noah's flood marked the end of the prehistoric world and the re-birth of the new one and it is here where our history begins to flourish. David Rohl states:

"What we know from the Book of Genesis as the Noah's Flood was probably an historical event which took place not long before the appearance of wheel-thrown pottery and writing in the ancient Near East. This catastrophic flood brought an end to the Ubiad culture and acted as a catalyst for the rapid development of civilisation -----."

"----- archaeology suggests the date of the catastrophic flood occurred some time in the fourth millennium BC. **8**

Shortly after this period migrating tribes appeared in Europe, Africa and further towards the Far East taking with them their advances in civilisation and technology. They also took with them their stories and legends.

"H.S. Bellamy in *Moons, Myths and Men* estimates that altogether there are over 500 Flood legends worldwide. Ancient civilizations such as (China, Babylonia, Wales, Russia, India, America, Hawaii, Scandinavia, Sumatra, Peru, and Polynesia) all have their own versions of a giant flood. These flood tales are frequently linked by common elements that parallel the Biblical account including the warning of the coming flood, the construction of a boat in advance, the storage of animals, the inclusion of family, and the release of birds to determine if the water level had subsided. The overwhelming consistency among flood legends found in distant parts of the globe indicates they were derived from the same origin (the Bible's record), but oral transcription has changed the details through time". **9**

A publication of the Archaeological institute of America stated in July Aug 2003 that: "Iraq is not just a desert. It's the place where civilization began, it's the longest surviving continuous tradition of civilization in the world, it's earlier than Egypt, it's earlier than any place else. And that it is the foundation of all ideas of civilization, for Western civilization as well as Eastern. And that we trace our own cultural roots back to Mesopotamia." **10**

Similarly Ryan & Pitman through their extensive research carried out in and around the region of the Black Sea also claim:

"Mesopotamia's area within and between the Tigris and Euphrates rivers is said to be the cradle from which western civilisation sprang" – which is a powerful thought. **11**

This is further re-enforced by Bill Cooper's highly detailed research which brilliantly traces ancient civilization of Britain and Europe back to Japheth, son of Noah! [12]

According to Genesis human life on planet earth had become so wicked and vile that Noah's flood came as a direct judgement from God. Eight surviving family members of Noah, destined to restart a new civilisation, are therefore our most recent and traceable original ancestors.

However in our pursuit of our origins we must go back further to the very root of human behaviour, to the Garden of Eden, Adam and Eve and the first bite of the "apple".

What ! A Talking Snake ?

"Well I don't really believe in that Garden of Eden stuff an' all that. It's just a myth. I mean how can you have a talking snake?" ---

Is the usual comment.

Adam & Eve seal discovery.3500 BC [13]

Well hang on a minute! Haven't you ever been into a pet-shop and heard a parrot speak.

And can you remember the talking dog on the adverts that could say "sozziges", and wasn't Balaam's Donkey supposed to speak? In any case communication with species doesn't necessarily have to use words. - Barbara Woodhouse became quite famous during the '80's with her ability to communicate with animals in demonstration of that. In reality, the account in the Garden of Eden illustrates how mankind was originally fooled by the trickery of a counterfeit deity.

The encounter in Genesis chapter two involves the supernatural, and although the serpent's subtle character is well depicted the practical realities of this event run much deeper.

Satan is seen as one who "transforms himself into an angel of light in order to deceive" (2 Cor.11:14) and here the serpent, Hebrew word *Nachesh* possibly originally meaning a *shining, enchanting being,* seems a good description.

The idea of a serpent is not seen simply as a talking snake with symbolic significance alone, but the highest of all angels, an anointed cherub who five times claims he will "ascend to my throne above the stars of God -- and be like the most high." (Isa.14:13). Here he states a half-lie and gives a pantheistic view that God is in everything and that you too can be like Him. After all you are in His image etc. Nachesh seems, to Eve, to represent God, therefore he can be believed. Lucifer, this *light bearer*, "son of the morning"(Isa.14:12-15) is very attractive and seductive with hypnotic musical charm. If an angel appearing in a burning bush could cause Moses to remove his shoes, how could Eve, in her ignorance, possibly resist such a majestic form? This was not some ugly monstrosity with horns and a forked tail; that may have scared her off. No, the spectre must have been attractive and charming.

Temptation is usually directed against body, soul or spirit, however in Eve's case it was against all three. The fruit of the tree was "good for food", so appealing to bodily needs, "pleasant to the eyes" by appealing to the emotions, and appealing to the mind and spirit by offering to "make one wise". One can understand how such *nachesh* could be revered as a deity. Unfortunately Eve did not recognise that "all that is in the world – the lust of the flesh, the lust of the eyes, and the pride of life is not of the Father". (1John.1:16) How co-incidental it is that apparitions of powerful spectres throughout the ages have had a similar effect and sometimes even created a following. Cults and 'isms such as those found in paganism, witchcraft and many distorted imitations of Christianity often try to portray the omnipotent, omniscient, omnipresent God naturally represented in all aspects of nature with its elves, pixies, goblins and all. Dr Henry Morris; former president of the *Institute of Creation Research* has this to say:

"Many New Age and other pantheistic cults have adopted Lucifer as their god". 14

The enemy, Satan, would love to see a weak church full of wishy-washy Christians who no longer believe the Bible as the inspired Word of God. There is no room for compromise - and that begins with Genesis!
I frequently refer to this quote from Ephesians 6:12. which tells us in no uncertain terms:

"For we wrestle not against flesh and blood, but against principalities, against powers, against the rulers of the darkness of this world, against spiritual wickedness in high places".

We are told in Genesis that Eden's life source was the "Tree of Life", a star-gate that was continually open providing both God's presence and communication with His creation. Whilst ever this link remained intact everything would be perfect as God intended. Unfortunately as we read it was not to last. Man disobeyed and the life-source withdrew in consequence. However symbolic we may interpret this, man through his independence had chosen to go it alone and had unknowingly left himself wide open to forces he had not accounted for. And the guarding cherubs were made well aware that Heaven's *star-gate* was now well and truly closed.

The new god

We read in Genesis 1:28 that God gave authority to man, meaning he had rights and responsibility for the care of planet earth and all its creation. But when he was hood-winked by the devil he forfeited those rights by allowing a counterfeit to share control. "The god of this world" (2 Cor.4:4. John12:31). "The ruler of the air". (Eph. 2:2) The thief who subtly sneaks in to steal and destroy (John 10:10) had now gained citizenship as a welcomed member of earth. "Without firing a shot" one might say he "walked right in through the front door" sat down and very quickly assumed command.

Eden's paradise had been perfectly designed. No pain, suffering, hardship or disease was God's intention, with man and his Creator living in mutual harmony. The only requirement from God was that of loyalty and obedience. The Genesis project had been put in place "and God saw that it was very good". But it was soon to change. Man naively seeing the opportunity to be independent and wise with false hope to be like a god, took the bait, only to discover he had not only disobeyed God but by such an act had handed over to Satan the right of access. What can only be described as an abuse of the Divine gift of freewill resulted in the greatest mistake in history! Eve's succumbing to temptation is not so much the stealing of an "apple", or more accurately put the forbidden fruit, but rather a simple act of rebellion. And as the Bible so aptly puts it: "Rebellion is as the sin of witchcraft" (1 Sam.15: 23) and witchcraft is the religion of devil worship.

Paradise was exchanged for knowledge and knowledge without responsibility and guidance is a recipe for disaster. Knowledge that would have been gained in due time, as man and his Creator walked hand in hand, had now been taken, ravaged and used for selfish gain in what was to become the brave new world of the *survival of the fittest.*

As God now withdrew from His immediate relationship with Adam and Eve and the Garden of Eden in all its splendour, the spiritual vacuum was quickly filled with the presence of evil and its manifest corruption of God's Creation, and so the struggle began under a new world order.

Conclusion

The evidence for the existence of Eden being an actual geographical place at some-time in the ancient past is overwhelming.

Although its precise locality and social structure is subject to much debate, most academics agree that it existed somewhere in the region of the Tigris and Euphrates rivers, in what is now modern day Iraq and Iran.

It is also claimed by a large number of historians and scholars that every race on earth owes its origin to somewhere in this general area of the Middle East, although the topography would have changed drastically due to Noah's flood.

Based on the above facts, the biblical account of Adam and Eve being the first of human civilisation becomes a powerful consideration. This being the case the Bible's explanation for the existence of evil and suffering through man's "original sin" has to be a natural conclusion.

Notes and References

1. Temptation Seal. British Museum. *Post-Akkadian, about 2200 to 2100 BC*
From Mesopotamia The tree, serpent and figures carved on this greenstone cylinder seal suggested to George Smith, an Assyriologist working in the British Museum between 1840 and 1876, that the scene was related to the Old Testament story of the temptation of Eve in the Garden of Eden. In fact, the seal shows a scene that is common on seals of the twenty-third and twenty-second centuries BC, with a seated male figure (identified by his head-dress of horns as a god) facing a female worshipper. The date palm between them and the snake may be symbolic of fertility. Although the British museum give their conservative opinion as to its connection with the Book of Genesis, there are many who through sound research would have a more positive opinion, for example Bill Cooper and of course Assyriologist George Smith himself.

2. David Rohl. "Legend. The Genesis of Civilization". [London: Random House (Century Press). 1998], P.66.

3. Tas Walker . Creation Ministries International (CMI). 24th Jan.2001.

4. Juris Zarins claimed to locate Eden now submerged in the northern end of the Persian Gulf. - -Wikipedia. 2013

5 Rohl "legend" p 67

6 "The Bibles Hidden secrets". BBC. Television series. March.2012. Dr Franchesc Stavrakopoulou made typical generalisations about ancient Israel and the Mid. East - Nothing new.

7 Ancient Sumerian tablet discovered during the latter part of the nineteenth century by the university of Pennsylvania. Translated by Herman Hilprecht, he dated this to around 2100 BC and believed it to be a very early record of the flood. Because this precedes the Babylonian records of much later, known as the *Epic of Gilgamesh*, it more accurately confirms today's Genesis record. - http://www.icr.org/article/genesis-gilgamesh-early-flood-tablet

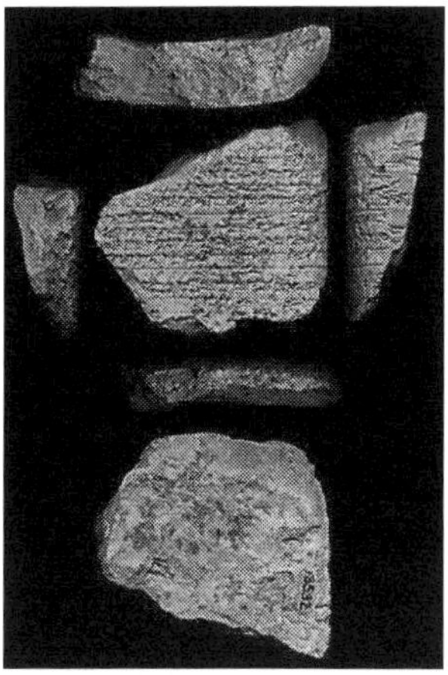

8 Rohl "Legend". P.177&180.

9 http://www.nwcreation.net/noahlegends.html/ 2013-12-14

10 http://archive.archaeology.org/0307/etc/civilization.html 2013-12-14

11 Ryan &Pitman . "Noah's Flood". (New York: Simon & Shuster. 1998), P.197. Fascinating scientific research by Drs. Ryan &Pitman confirming the catastrophic flooding of the Black sea area of Mesopotamia coinciding with the recorded Biblical event.

12 Bill Cooper. "After the Flood". (Chichester: New Wine Press, 1995). Excellent work based on 25 years research confirming the Biblical ancestry of the whole of European civilization.

13 In 1932 E. A. Speiser of the University Museum of Pennsylvania discovered a seal near the bottom of the Tepe Gawra Mound twelve miles from Nineveh. He estimated that the seal came from about 3500 B.C. It shows a naked man and a naked woman, both bent over as if they were oppressed or downcast. Behind them, partly broken, is a serpent (see drawing in upper left of image).
The seal is small, only about one inch in diameter, engraved on stone, and is now held in the University Museum in Pennsylvania. Speiser pointed out, the image on the seal is strongly suggestive of the Adam and Eve story. http://www.bible-archaeology.info/adam.htm

14 Dr. Henry Morris. "New Defender's Bible". (Nashville: World Publishing, 2006), P.1026.

Chapter 6.

The Conflict.

"Nothing is easier than to admit in words the truth of the universal struggle for life". Charles Darwin. 1.

Dave was an old guy who walked around Chesterfield homeless, not in the best of health, crippled from arthritis plus years of abuse and

general buffeting that life can often inflict. He was a regular at the charity soup kitchens, mission bus and even occasionally church, particularly during evenings when food was part of the service. Dave was a man who was to say the least not easy to get on with. His aggressive attitude often caused people to resent him, and sometimes he would finish up being beaten and robbed of what little "State benefit" he might have left in his grimy pockets. A sad little man with no hope, like the proverbial snowball in hell he was one day found half frozen in some shop doorway, his last resort in a desperate attempt to beat off the harsh winter bite. Yet in spite of all this whilst he was alive he still maintained some pride. Maybe not pride in himself as any self-respect had disappeared long ago - but pride in the fact that for some reason he had to keep going even if it was for the weekly post office pay-out and the reward it gave him of buying another bottle of cider; his favourite diet and often the highlight of the week. When things really got to him he'd wind up in jail for a night or two, a kind of respite or change of scenery if you like. Being thrown out of a temporary accommodation (which the council might have found him during sub-zero climate) for bad behaviour or urinating in a shop doorway was his usual passport to a spot of "home comfort" and in some cases a longer spell in Her Majesty's Hotel. Dave probably also kept going for another reason: that maybe there was hope. He'd often chatted with many Christian volunteer workers in town, some whose piety would grate on his broken spirit, but there would be those who in-spite of Dave's awkward and sometimes aggressive backlash would get through to him. Earning Dave's respect was a skill that only a few could manage but somehow he listened. His Biker's Bible, his odd bottle of cider and maybe a few understanding friends on the weekly Church Army mission bus was about all the comfort he had, the rest was hardship. **2**

I recall one snowy night many years ago when the mission bus broke down at the most awkward of places. Chaos, drunks, F-words and vomit rained on, plus an audience of on-lookers, whilst waiting for the break-down truck to arrive. Dave sitting in the epicentre absolutely refused to move because where he was it was nice and warm! Needless to say a riot was almost added to the list. Dave is one of thousands if not millions of suffering mortals on this planet whose lot is nothing more than a very good slice of bad luck. Some of it may be self-inflicted but often it isn't. I'd like to believe Dave's thread of Divine hope helped him and that because of his mustard grain of faith we'll see him in Heaven one day, God only knows. What I do feel sure of is that Dave would rather have gone through his hardship on earth with his friend Jesus than without him, and that's the difference!

On reading this story in the light of the quotation at the chapter heading, one might appreciate that Darwin's observation of the struggle for existence within nature, including our own species, was extremely accurate:

"We behold its face bright with gladness and often see a superabundance of food; we do not see or we forget that the birds that are idly singing around us mostly live on insects or seeds and are thus constantly destroying life".3.

Yet this fight for survival doesn't stop with birds, bees, plants and trees, it extends to the whole of life, even human. The difference seems to be that whereas nature has provided sufficient for all, there are those who want more. Greed and selfish desire seem to be more attributable to humankind than certain primates. In our arrogance we laugh and poke fun at the chimp in the zoo, peg our noses when orang-utans daub each other with excrement, yet at times we are no better and in fact we can be far worse. We're very good also at blaming the planet for her track record of sometimes not being too benevolent towards its inhabitants. We know only too well that when she lashes out in anger nature can be pretty fierce as any volcanic eruption, earthquake or flood will tell us. But our greatest sorrow, as Robert Burns once said, is Man's inhumanity to his brother:

"Why do we hunt and persecute each other? Why is our world so full of man's infamous inhumanity to man - and to woman?" **4.**

Millions of people, like our friend Dave, have learned the hard way that this end of *nature* can be extremely cruel.

When Darwin visited the Fuegian islands, on the southernmost tip of South America, his observations of what he perceived as their gross barbaric culture left him appalled at the fact that here were so called humans who hadn't even the basic civilized codes of behaviour of a half decent ape. From his observations he could only conclude that here was evidence of nothing short of a reversion to the one time primate state which he believed was ancestral in all *Homo sapiens* (i.e. us) and could therefore support his theory of evolution.

"For my own part I would as soon be descended from that heroic little monkey, who braved his dreaded enemy in order to save the life of his keeper, or from that old baboon, who descending from the mountains, carried away in triumph his young comrade from a crowd of astonished dogs -- - as from a savage who delights in the torture of his enemies, offers up bloody sacrifices, practices infanticide without remorse, treats his wives like slaves, knows no decency, and is haunted by the grossest superstitions."**5.**

When considering this at its face value there's little wonder that the humanists feel justified at taking a good swing at God

Red in tooth and claw.

Originally coined by Lord Alfred Tennyson, nature's struggle for existence through "red in tooth and claw" is true indeed and at face value Darwin's monochrome observation is nothing more than a stating of the obvious. But why might we ask? Why would a God of love create a world full of so much struggle and hardship? The Bible's answer is; He didn't. The Creator of the Universe whose "thoughts and ways are not man's thoughts" (Isa.55:8) had a better idea. What Darwin interpreted as "a reversion to the one time primate state", which he believed is ancestral in all *Homo sapiens*, the Bible calls the effect of original sin. When we compare the image of Adam, the fulfilment of God's Creation in all his splendour, with that of the savage as described by Darwin, there is a world of difference. When Adam abused his God given right of free will and allowed Satan right of access to planet earth, Satan, the devil brought with him all his dirt and baggage, resulting in a withdrawal of God's life sustaining light. It is vital to grasp that this polluting sin which radiates from a satanic source of evil was and still is the cause of so much grotesque distortion and corruption we have witnessed on earth throughout history. However God would not be God if He didn't see this coming, and He knew from the beginning of time that this would be the case. After all He is "Alpha and Omega, the beginning and the end" (Rev.22:13). There is therefore no doubt that into the DNA of life the Creator would have fixed in place latent defence mechanisms that when the survival of the fittest kicked-in at the Fall of Man and consequent infection of sin, life would survive, adapt and still pro-create and fill the Earth despite struggle and opposition. The Lion, the bear, the snake, the honey bee and many more were thus empowered, and the battle was on! For Man as well as beast there is no exception: "For everything there is a season and a purpose under Heaven. A time to be born and a time to die --- -a time for war and a time for peace" (Eccl.3:1) Also;"a time to beat swords into ploughshares" (Isa.ch.2:4) but also a time to "beat ploughshares back into swords."(Joel.3:10). Unfortunately there have been those throughout history like Hitler and other proponents of the eugenics movement who not only twisted this fact of life but by believing they could give "natural selection" a helping hand took the whole thing a leap forward. The world knows only too well what Hitler's version of social Darwinism believed:

"Those who want to live, let them fight, and those who do not want to fight in this world of eternal struggle do not deserve to live,"

Viewed in this light it can only be seen as Darwin's dangerous idea. **6**

Since Darwin, evolutionary philosophy has had a profound influence on most of the liberal arts and social sciences of our day. For example, one can't fail to notice when reading Darwin's; "The Origin of Species" and later book "The Descent of Man", that there exists strong emphasis on favoured "races", or rather varieties of species as Darwin explained. Ideas that today would be criticised, (or at best misunderstood) as being racist, have had a great influence on certain political philosophies in recent times. Many researchers now believe the philosophies of Hitler, Marx, Mao, and others gained much inspiration from this source of Darwinian thought. Some also recognize that traces of this have helped to form a basis of a type of secular humanism that has completely changed our country from having traditional beliefs that were healthy for our nation, to a postmodern belief system that is having a devastating effect on all aspects of our lives today. Ironically one might conclude that instead of trying to explain the cause of suffering, evolution has in fact help create some of its own.

The early years

Since Darwin first published *The Origin of Species* in 1859 the worldview on our ancestry took on a whole new understanding. The concept of long ages and gradual evolution of life from one form to another was becoming popular amongst scientific thinkers of the day. Although nothing new (in fact the idea of evolution dates back to the ancient Greeks. 7), evolution as the birth or rather re-birth of an old philosophical idea was to be spawned in the mind of Charles Darwin's grandfather, Erasmus. Inspired also by scientific thinkers of his era such as Charles Lyell and James Hutton who had developed ideas associated with earth geology being millions of years old and not thousands, Charles stood great on giant's shoulders. But then one cannot ignore his genius and passion plus intense research which earned him a place amongst the great scientists of the past. One also has to admire his boldness in the face of much opposition from the established church, which of course defended with equal passion the biblical view of a six day creation and a young earth.

Ironically Charles Darwin was not a trained scientist in the modern sense, least of all a biologist.

After giving up on medical school at Edinburgh he turned to the study of theology. Earning his degree at Cambridge, it put him on track to become a clergyman. But direction changed again when he was given the chance to join the five year voyage on HMS Beagle – a golden opportunity for this young naturalist. Because of his passion for natural science most of his biological and botanical knowledge was gained through his own research and study, much to his deserved credit. Unfortunately for subsequent devotees of neo-Darwinism, large flaws in his theory have intellectually blinded many a good scientist and theologian.

For example the Interpreter's Bible:

"A commentary set that came into the mainline churches like a tidal wave, was dominated by writers who assigned Genesis to the realm of myth. Men like Walter Russell Bowie (who would influence a young Jack Spong- (*a vehement opponent of biblical authenticity*) introduced the subtly blasphemous idea that the Bible was influenced by Babylonian myth. This teaching opened up an assault on the Christian faith that has only intensified." **8**

During a speaking trip to England in recent times, Professor John Rendle-Short (Chairman emeritus, Creation Ministries International Australia) told a group of pastors that if they rejected a literal Genesis in favour of evolutionary ideas (or even just millions of years), this would put them on a slippery slide of unbelief:

"If we re-interpret God's Word in Genesis to fit man's fallible opinion, then ultimately, it would only be consistent to apply this same hermeneutic (method of interpretation) elsewhere—even to Christ's Resurrection". **9**

It was only a matter of time and shift of paradigm fashion before the established church of Darwin's day caved-in to a somewhat "peaceful" compromise. Lyell's agenda "To free science from Moses" seemed to be happening. Darwin of course had already made his decision. After suffering the loss of his young daughter his faith in God and any thoughts of the priesthood slowly ebbed away, leaving him to devote the rest of his life to his passion for natural sciences.

Evolution can be believed?

In most people's understanding, the theory of evolution is the gradual development of species over a long period of time consisting of millions of years. What we are not so easily told, is that the "long time" theory is based on the accurate dating of rocks, which according to Dr Monty White, "is meaningless", and is a problem for evolutionists. The mainspring to all this and to what makes it tick is ***natural selection,*** or the weeding out of the weak in favour of the strong. Herbert Spencer first coined the phrase; "The survival of the fittest" in 1864 after reading Darwin's *Origin of Species*.

The process of selection, through either selective breeding or natural fight for survival against extinction, creates vast variations in certain species. However, to claim that this has been the means by which all life has been selected causing microbes to develop into man, and because it has never been proven, it remains only a "theory", or rather a hypothesis as some scientists might more finely describe it. The idea of "goo to you via the zoo" is no better than a child's "Just so Story" and only provides fuel for atheistic belief. When we hear rhetoric like "the evidence for evolution is overwhelming" we're sold a package and in that package is a certain amount of truth. Yes of course natural selection is a fact; we see it in daily competition, from the business and sports world to the animal kingdom. Variation and adaptation within species exists, which may allow for one species to change into another, but it cannot change the *genus* or "kind", which is where it makes the false claim. For example we don't get elephants changing into monkeys, nor monkeys changing into man, because their genus is entirely different. Sometimes we might hear science use terms like micro and macro evolution to distinguish between the small developments within species (micro) and what is hypothesised to be a large development or leap (macro) from one genus to another. But this can be misleading by making us think that by calling the *variations* micro *evolution* we have to assume that *all* evolution is a fact and therefore the same thing. The small variations do not evolve, they are instead acting in result of design- and that implies a designer- not random chance. The problem is once the word "evolution" has found its way into our thoughts it's hard to get rid of it. So within the package is crafted the idea of ***natural selection acting upon random mutations to produce life***. In other words Darwinian natural selection has caused life to exist without the need of a creator, and the evidence for that is ***not*** overwhelming, in fact it's non-existent! However it's too late - the bait has been taken and the dummy sold, and the old adage is probably right:

"A lake of truth with a pint of poison is the devil's best trick". He is an excellent salesman! Sadly this is now global; bought by many and well seated in our educational system. Yet evolution is the religion of atheism and atheism is anti-God.

The religion of evolution is now so powerful and so vehemently preached by its high priests of atheism, often under the flag of Life Sciences, that when poured through the sacred altar of television, the average man in the street, like Eve in the garden, has no chance but to swallow it hook line and sinker. Yet when packaged in such a way it can only be described as the greatest lie in history, or as Jonathan Sarfati in his book refers to it as the "Greatest Hoax on Earth". – Recommended reading.

Furthermore Susan Mazur unveils some startling facts in her book *"The Altenburg 16; Expose' of the Evolution Industry"*, which gives the strong impression that the future of the theory of Darwinian evolution looks pretty bleak. She claims:

"Evolutionary science is as much about the posturing, salesmanship, stonewalling and bullying that goes on as it is about actual scientific theory. It is a social discourse involving hypotheses of staggering complexity with scientists, recipients of the biggest grants of any intellectuals, assuming the power of politicians whilst engaged in animal house pie-throwing and name-calling: "ham fisted", "looney Marxist hangover, "secular creationist", "philosopher" (a scientist who can't get grants anymore), "quack", "crackpot". " **10**

It seems therefore that Susan Mazur would have us conclude that evolution is not so much a search for the truth as a search for the next grant.

"In short, it's a modern day quest for the holy grail but with few knights" **11**

She states how a wave of scientists now question natural selection's role although few will publicly admit it. What can only be described as a high level interwoven web of politics and squandered government cash, all in the name of science, frankly leave most political leaders clueless as to what evolution is about anyway. Mazur adds how the result is the intellectual starvation of children due to "outdated books and unenlightened teachers". In reality the thread throughout the book tells us that Darwin has had his day and science is now desperate for a new theory of origins.

Anything but Creation!

The following is a recent extract from Creation Magazine April 2013:-

It should be evident to most that there are indeed powerful forces at work in the world today acting to "suppress the truth". This often starts very young, especially in government schools, and even church schools.

In line with this, we received this letter from a grandmother some years ago:

Grandson Jacob's teacher gave the 'party line' on origins yesterday.

"Two massive clouds of cosmic gases collided and as a result our sun emerged ..."
Jacob raised his hand and interrupted, "I don't believe that!"

"I beg your pardon, Jacob? Why not?" she asked.

"Because there was nothing but GOD and He just spoke and that's where our sun came from," was the simple faith of this 8-year-old.

The teacher responded: "You know, I don't believe it [evolution] either.

Jacob, you are right. It happened just like you said but I'm not allowed to say it [creation] as a teacher. Thank you for saying it for me."

.

This is no isolated case. On hearing the story, another Australian teacher said: "
"Yes! That's exactly how it is at my school, too. The principal read the 'riot act' out to us in the staff room: no mentioning creation in class, unless one of the kids ... [raises] the issue." **12**

When I read stories like this, frankly, I am stunned! What on earth are they doing to our kids? How dare they accuse Christians of brainwashing when "All things bright and beautiful" is replaced with "All things politically correct"? And the God of Creation is exchanged for the creation of a god, who must not be challenged for fear of getting the sack! If education is about discovery and investigation then how can one freely learn truth when being blinkered by such party-line bigotry! *They*, these potentates of education whom we trust to shape our children's minds, accuse us of indoctrination yet in their own failure they indoctrinate ignorance. Surely if you don't encourage young people to question then won't they do it anyway? Isn't this how we discover, and how we invent, improve and help create a better world to live in? Don't they know that pioneers of science in the past wrought science and discovery through their recognition of a Creator. Don't they also know that pioneers of social reform and equality dedicated their services to mankind because of their Christian faith? Don't they know that many of the great artists painted from a heart – fired by faith, and designers copied and created designs already found in Creation! Weren't *they* once taught that we're also created in God's image? Yet *they* want to rob us of this heritage by saying we're all "Darwin's monkeys"! Is there any wonder that some people grow up to behave like them?

Some, in their entrusted leadership, even accuse Christians of believing in some kind of ghoulish God yet they create one far worse, in fact they create many. I imagine many such opponents of Christianity have probably never been to church, never read a Bible and haven't a clue what being a Christian is all about. In their arrogance of ignorance they mock, control and create empires and icons in their own "pagan" world!

Facing the challenge

Our present generation, with its climate of rapid changes, is witnessing increasing attacks on Christianity. The focus on Genesis and the subject of origins has never been more important during the last 150 years of Darwinism as it is now. Christianity in the UK as some of us are well aware is being marginalized and in some cases openly allowed to be ridiculed. The very foundation of our faith in God as Creator and Redeemer, including our historic cultural heritage is being eroded by secularism and militant atheism, and as in Paul's day the time is probably right to pick up the gauntlet of opportunity. There are hundreds if not thousands of scientists worldwide who have either personally or publicly (sometimes at the expense of their job) renounced traditional Darwinian evolutionary theory in favour of Intelligent Design and/or literal six day Creation worldviews.

Dr A C McIntosh claims:

" --- there is a growing body of professional ,educated opinion which does not accept atheistic humanism and its portrayal of evolution as a fact. Often it is a startling revelation to many sincere thinking people that there is any other way of thinking!". **13**.

This goes to show that it is not scientific evidence which is in dispute but its human interpretation and consequent worldviews. Christians now have access to good evidence supported by some excellent scientific networks of researchers who are passionate and are willing to help churches in their call to re-establish the gospel, that:

"We might always be prepared to make a defence to anyone who asks you for a reason for the hope that is in you." (1Peter.3:15) .

Much of this evidence for a young earth comes from a variety of scientific disciplines –physics, chemistry, geology, astronomy, and biology— easily accessible through the growing number of creation research institutions, which although often blocked by media control, can always be found on the web.

Christians have no need to fear the arch enemies of the church who wield the big stick of evolution with clever argument and skilled rhetoric. People like Richard Dawkins for example are in reality stirring us all up, believers and non-believers alike towards debate, study and research, and are ironically doing the church a favour.

Christianity is in no way unfamiliar with harsh threat, criticism, debate or even persecution; the past 2000 years have shown that. We read in the New Testament that the apostle Paul himself was a skilled defender of the faith and was very much at home when arguing with the Greek philosophers of his day in the debating arena. In fact we sometimes get the idea that he almost welcomed the challenge when reading accounts in the book of Acts of the Apostles. The fact is that Paul was so confident in his faith that he saw such opposing arguments not as a threat to the gospel but more of an opportunity to reveal it.

And if we believe as Christians we have truth on our side; then as it was in Paul's day the truth will prevail.

Dr. Henry Morris said that "Genesis is probably the most important book ever written", and that these are the stories which form the very root of our culture and accurately describe the history of the beginnings of civilization on this planet, give us reason for our existence, present condition and the hope for our future. **14**

The devil, Satan (name meaning "accuser") will have us believe that we are all accidents arising from some pre-historic slime that has neither soul nor purpose, and our ultimate goal is to procreate and to be finally recycled on the dung heap for useful compost! Therefore if we are to be clear of our purpose and ultimate destiny, and have a confident understanding of the rest of the Bible we need to get Genesis right!

Genesis gives us a choice

Freedom of choice usually carries its own responsibility and why God chose us to be so close to monkeys in our design is a mystery. What is plain however is the fact that we are spiritual animals with a capacity and sensitivity to embrace higher moral instincts. However our personal spiritual path may not necessarily be the same as that of another. There are those whose lifestyle is so wicked that they not only seem to have reverted back to animalistic instincts but have become far worse, in that they have embarked on nothing more than the path of evil. Darwin's honest observations –*The Descent of Man*– p 69 has shown such characteristics.

On the other hand there are many positive lifestyles and patterns of living to be observed on our planet and every one, I believe, is grounded in some belief system which gives it its drive. In the past much of our civilized world has been influenced by the Judeo-Christian belief pattern in one form or another aimed at striving to help create a better world and healthier attitudes. Yet in spite of its pioneering spirit, there has often been opposition from the world's darker side.

There seems therefore to be two extremes: Either the way of the world, i.e. the survival of the fittest proving ourselves to be better than the next man wallowing in a dog-eat-dog world of ducking and diving, only to discover that sooner or later we get wiped out like our prehistoric ancestor, or following what seems to be a higher way; the way of Grace – the Jesus pattern.

We cannot escape the fact that within just about every human relationship or connection sooner or later we get the opportunity to put this one to the test. Such "higher qualities" as tolerance, forgiveness, humility and compassion, I believe are all part of the "grace package" which gets called into play through daily living.

How much of it we choose to apply of course is up to us. However one certainty is this: that if planet Earth is to survive for any length of time it has to learn this one pretty quick, because the global alternative is unthinkable!

Therefore:

"Enter in at the narrow gate: for wide is the gate, and broad is the way, that leads to destruction, and many there be who go in there. For the gate is small and the way is narrow that leads to life, and there are few who find it". (Matt.7:13-14)

Conclusion

Although the "universal struggle for life" is plain for all to see, it is better understood as the "whole of nature waiting for its redemption" as described in the New Testament. And "what we now see only as a reflection in a mirror one day we shall see face to face" (1Cor.13:12)

The Bible's worldview states that the origin of conflict is spiritual and constantly highlights the opposing forces of evil against good. (Eph. 6:10-18).

The history of planet earth has often shown justification for wars and physical force in an attempt to overcome evil. The biblical worldview is to "overcome evil with good" as shown by Jesus in his demonstration of God's grace.

Notes and References.

1. Charles Darwin, “Origin of Species”. (London: Wordsworth Editions, 1998), p,49.

2. Mission Bus: Better known as “Church on the Bus” A specific ministry to the homeless in Chesterfield and Matlock areas serving emotional, physical and spiritual needs. Originated and presently served by Capt. Alan Park since 2005. Photograph by courtesy of Church Army.

3. Charles Darwin, “Origin of Species”, p,50..

4. "Man's inhumanity to man" is first documented in the Robert Burns poem called Man was made to mourn: A Dirge in 1784. It is possible that Burns re-worded a similar quote from Samuel von Pufendorf who in 1673 wrote, "More inhumanity has been done by man himself than any other of nature's causes." From Wikipedia, the free encyclopaedia.

5. Charles Darwin, “The Descent of Man”. [London: Penguin Group Publishers. (Plume Book Science) 2007] , p.415

6. The damning words of Adolf Hitler which just about sums up the rest of his chapter on "Race and People",ch.11 of "Mein Kampf". It is interesting to note how one can't help but sense a strong distorted echo of Darwin's "Origin of species" or "The Descent of man" when reading Hitler's text.

> Also William Dembski, intelligent design creationist and co-author of *Moral Darwinism*, claims:
>
> "Darwin is the founder of the modern eugenics movement in all its later myriad forms, whether it is expressed through a call to weed out the unfit, breed more of the fit, abort the undesirable and deformed or manipulate our nature genetically through technology"
>
> Furthermore; physician Ernst Haeckel after reading Darwin's *Origin of Species*. used it as ammunition to attack religious dogma and to build his own world view.
>
> Stephen Jay Gould's "Ontology and Phylogeny": "Haeckel's evolutionary racism; his call to the German people for racial purity and unflinching devotion to a "just" state; his belief that harsh, inexorable laws of evolution ruled human civilization and nature alike, conferring upon favored races the right to dominate others . . . all contributed to the rise of Nazism. ----

--Cited in "Darwin's connection to Nazi Eugenics Exposed". Science Blogs.com July 14. 2009.

7. Writers of the early church age often had mixed interpretations for Gen.1, some of which were "*literal, figurative or unclear*" . Origen for example, textual scholar of the Alexandrian School,185-253 AD, whose work often bordered on heresy, could still be viewed as a "young earth creationist". His time span for Creation however was about 10,000 BC as opposed to *circa*.5,500 BC claimed by Biblical scholars such as "*Clement, Julius, Hippolytus Eusebius and Augustine of Hippo*". In Greek philosophy Anaximander (610-540 BC) believed man had developed from fish and Empedocles took Man's origin further back to plants. Aristotle however classified all living organisms in a hierarchical chain of being (with possible slight resemblance to Darwin's "tree of life") with plants at the bottom, then animals, to finally Man as the pinnacle of creation. Later Augustine by accommodating certain Greek ideas was to show God as Designer with things having place and purpose. – Jonathan Sarfati. "Refuting Compromise".2004:121-122. Master Books, Green Forest.

8. Ken Ham. "Why Won't They Listen". (Green forest. USA : Master Books), p,150.

9. Ken Ham & Stacia Byers. AIG. June 1; 2000. "The slippery slide to unbelief" .

WWW. Allaboutcreation.org. 2013-12-14

10. Susan Mazur, "The Altenburg 16; Expose' of the Evolution Industry (Berkeley California, North Atlantic Books, 2010), Introduction, pp.v.

11. Ibid

12. Creation Magazine April 2013.Vol 35 No3 Article: "Winning against suppression " P,6

13. Dr Andy McIntosh, former professor of Thermodynamics. Leeds University. "Genesis for today" (Leominster: Day One publications. 2001), P10

Also highly recommended further reading:-

"Evolution Impossible" – Dr. John Ashton, PhD – Master Books, 2012, Green Forest, AR.

"Buried Alive" – the untold story about Neanderthal Man – Jack Cuozzo. 2008, Master Books, Green Forest.

14. Dr. Henry Morris. "The Genesis Record". (Grand Rapids: Baker Publishing. 2007), p,17.

"Church on the Bus" project founded by Church Army Capt. Alan Park – Chesterfield.

Chapter 7

Hawking's Universe ----

-----"Much ado about nothing"

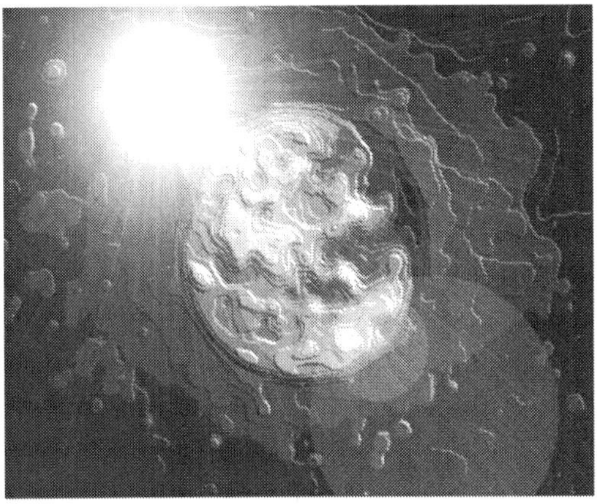

"We take the side of science (naturalistic) in spite of the patent absurdity of some of its constructs---- in spite of the tolerance of the scientific community for un-substantiated "just so stories", because we have an a priori commitment to materialism---- and that materialism is an absolute for we cannot allow a divine foot in the door."

Professor Richard Lewontin. 1.

William Sanderson's story is indeed remarkable. To some it's one of many heard before, to others it's just "pie in the sky". It's not every day we come across stories like this, and sometimes it's all too easy to either get lost in the clouds, or throw the book in the bin in some premature conclusion that it's a load of old rubbish. When occasions like this occur it's sometimes good to air a few balanced views in order to get some kind of "earthing".

Sometimes a lot of damage to incredible accounts like this can be caused by Christians themselves. "Super-saints" I often call them, others might call them "Bible thumpers" - hurling themselves into your face armed with quotes and references only to leave their victims well cringed. Such people not only give Christians a bad name but often give the impression we're *all* nuts. Good ideas at some point need checks and balances and even more so, do spiritual ones. Saint Paul advised wise discernment by church leaders when dealing with spiritual issues, and he certainly knew what reality was! **2.** I'm sure during and after William Sanderson's miracle there would have been much discussion and ecclesiastical "chit-chat", but at the end of the day the facts spoke for themselves as William now stood before them! For our part, a century later, unfortunately our scientific age has so groomed us, that almost every act of living requires some scientific thought. From unblocking a sink waste-pipe to accessing a computer, science and technology are here to stay. It is for this reason that I believe that modern scientific thought must be considered when reading about such experiences as William Sanderson's. Although we may not all be scientific, our Western cultures have indeed indoctrinated us to question just about everything.

Grasp the nettle.

Stephen Hawking is hailed by many as the most famous living scientist of our time. Retired Cambridge Professor who held the highly revered chair once held by the great Sir Isaac Newton. There is of course little wonder that in the present climate of "New Atheism" headed by such "high priests" as Richard Dawkins, Hawking's final break from a God possibility for Creation has now added powerful fuel to their cause. It is because there seems to be a developing clique of hard-nosed scientists, who with great academic authority and status are hell-bent on getting rid of God, that I have decided to "grasp the nettle" and use Hawking's Universe as an example to merely represent, and indeed open up, this general attitude and mind-set that we're up against. Mark this however I am not pretending "Hawking cosmology" is something I can tackle. That would be silly, as professor Hawking is far too clever. Hawking explains his theories in simple terms so that the average person can take from it what he or she needs to know and that's what we have to work with. I feel sure that when reading his books his ultimate aim is to somehow wrench quantum physics from the unseen micro world to the world of every-day living in an attempt make it relevant to practical philosophy. After all his dream is that ordinary people as well as philosophers and scientists, will be able to take part in discussions about our existence in the universe. – see ref.8. This being the case he obviously wants us to weigh the evidence for ourselves. You don't have to be a lawyer to be able to make legal decisions as a member of a jury, because you have legal experts who advise and interpret the technicalities for you, and in the end it is the public representation which has to decide. In the same way you don't have to be a scientist, like Hawking, to examine some of his ideas and conclusions. So in this chapter our examination can be made palatable with the help from other good scientist's observations who do not share the same atheistic world-view. I am also a firm believer in the yardstick of common sense - a God given tool which we can all apply, because without such common sense it becomes nonsense, and "sometimes the simplest answer is the right one". 3.

Science or philosophy?

Some years ago (1980's) I read Professor Stephen Hawking's book; *A Brief History of time* and became quite fascinated by the amazing way he could simplify and put into layman's terms what would, due to its profound scientific depth, normally be way beyond the grasp of the man in the street. When conversing on subjects akin to the origin of the universe we usually have a quick stab at it based on our own meagre gleanings of bits of information – which of course can make us sound quite clever amongst those less informed – and then sharply move on to a more, and somewhat academically safer, philosophically based conclusion; this is usually when we end up with thoughts and theories about our own mortality. Home grown philosophy is something we can all relate to, after all philosophy is intended to be about reasons for being and the attempt to answer what we call first order questions: Where have we come from? Why are we here, and where we are going, etc? These are questions which man has pondered from day one and are part of the very fabric of our existence.

It's interesting to note however that in *A brief history of Time* professor Hawking doesn't let many pages of his book slip by without mentioning God, which seems to suggest that such an entity is either an important presence to consider in his science, or an irritating obstacle which might be in the way of his particular world-view.

On reading his second book *The Grand Design* (2012), he finally nails his colours to the mast by deciding that God must be taken off the scene altogether if we are to understand how the universe began. In other words there is no place for Him in Creation! Although I do find the last sentence a bit of a contradiction in terms, i.e. Creation implies a Creator which might be a brain teaser better handled by philosophy than science.

Unfortunately Hawking does not agree and tells us that:

"Traditionally these are questions for philosophy, but philosophy is dead. It has not kept up with modern developments in science, particularly physics. As a result scientists have become the bearers of discovery in our quest for knowledge". **4**

Yet in spite of this being his profound opinion I think it's only fair to say that within theoretical science/cosmology there is an awful lot of philosophy. *Even the above statement is in itself philosophical and is a statement about science rather than a statement of science - therefore contradictory.* **5** Any new or replacement philosophy which claims total reliance on physics needs to first realize that much of our science owes gratitude to philosophers of the past, from ancient Greeks to modern visionaries. Furthermore any new philosophy first has to work for the "lads on the shop-floor" – it has to have some practical every-day use. For example: will it relieve stress, alleviate suffering and hardship, give hope and faith etc ? If vectors, equations and whizzing particles are to be "sold" to Joe average then we've yet to see someone give us a product demonstration. This is usually where the rubber hits the road, and no matter how scientifically ingenious an idea might be, life will probably still clatter on in the same old way for a good while.

Of course William Sanderson's experience will naturally defy such reasoning as that offered by Professor Hawking, who of course is the scientist of the century and has very little time for religious explanations. However both their experiences do have some common ground: they are both unique and leave us with "cosmic" after-thoughts, and although they have a conflicting worldview, they might agree that both views contain a strong element of belief. It is because of this shared accord in the wonder of the "heavens" that I feel it would be good to first look at the "Grand order of things" from an earthly stance before heading off into a more Heavenly direction. William Sanderson's experience plus his message is of course a focal part of my book and of course is religious. This doesn't mean that anything that is heavenly minded is of no earthly use. On the contrary the ultimate aim of this book is to show the opposite, that a *living faith* is indeed vital.

Science or faith?

Sooner or later theoretical science like this which deals with origins of existence surely has to be coming from a faith_position. Not a faith in some supernatural deity but faith in a scientific belief system created by the ideas of man. **6 --** John MacKay –International Director, Creation Research.

Professor Hawking sets the scene by referring to four great fundamental forces of nature: the *strong* and *weak* nuclear forces, *electromagnetism* and *gravity.* **7** He ends on the note that if physicists were to ever find a theory that could unify all these forces together which he called *unification* or the "Theory of everything" –"then we would know the mind of God" **8**. He adds that "our goal is a complete understanding of the events around us, and of our own existence".**9** However in his later book; "The Grand Design" it is the laws of physics not the will of God that provide the real explanation as to how the universe came into being. The Big Bang was apparently the inevitable consequence of these laws. "Because there is a law of gravity the universe can and will create itself from nothing" he says. **10** Hawking's finale in writing his theory is that it is not God who is the grand designer but the laws of gravity acting through what he calls "spontaneous creation". **11** In other words the "nothing" at the so called beginning of everything was in fact "something" which immediately gives us the go ahead to claim that the something we now see all came from the nothing that we now don't see, which was really not nothing at all but something that we could probably call nothing! ---Got a headache yet! It gets worse. The "nothing" is apparently the presence of the laws of gravity (which now makes it something) which somehow have the power to cause the universe to create itself. Which is a bit like saying because we have the laws of mathematics then my monthly accounts will naturally look creatively healthy because at the end of the day theoretical figures can and will create cash!

Creation research scientist Dr Jake Herbert has this to say:

"Moreover, the general claim that the laws of physics could have created our universe suffers from a number of serious logical difficulties. Our understanding of the laws of physics is based on *observation*. For instance, our knowledge of the laws of conservation of momentum and energy come from observations made from literally thousands of experiments. No one has ever observed a universe "popping" into existence. This means that any laws of physics that would allow (even in principle) a universe to pop into existence are completely outside our experience. The laws of physics, as we know them, simply are not applicable here. Rather, the spontaneous creation of a universe would require higher "meta" or "hyper" laws of physics that might or might not be anything like the laws of physics that we know". **12**

And one could add that if a universe could simply "pop into existence" then what is it popping into? Whatever it "popped into" must also have existed first for it to get "popped"! And apparently when all that's said and done if we add all the sums up the answer is zero. I'll let Oxford professor; John Lennox explain:

"On the face of it Hawking appears, therefore to be asserting that the universe is created from nothing and from something – not a very promising start; ---what physicists refer to as a quantum vacuum, which is manifestly not nothing. Later on in his book he sets the total energy of empty space to zero by subtracting the actual value and then seems to proceed on the assumption that the energy actually is zero when he asks the question; "If the total energy of the universe is zero, and it costs energy to create a body, how can a whole universe be created from nothing?" "This seems, at least to me, a rather dubious move" **13**

Or rather; "much ado about nothing!"

Hawking's Universe

"We are always governed by our assumptions"---

-- "If a scientist does not believe in God, then his starting point of atheism will be bound to affect his judgment as he looks at the world around him. If his mind is closed to the possibility of a designer his own assumption will *force* him to adopt what to many will seem an 'unlikely' explanation for what he observes." – Professor Andy McIntosh. **14**

Now most of us are well familiar with the idea of "cause and effect". This pretty well established and well-tried law of physics - you know that which you were taught at school; "you can't get something from nothing". It's not only is a basic principle of science; namely the result of the 1st law of thermodynamics, but life in general. What I do find a bit worrying though is Hawking's philosophy seems to be trying to tell us that cause and effect could be a bit awkward now because it might imply that the universe has had a beginning. Such an idea of course would consequently mean someone or something might have started it, and we can't really allow a *Divine foot in the door,* can we? It seems he might have us believe that its ingredients, particles and forces have always been around, if not in this universe then some other. This might imply of course that the "big question" can be allowed to just go on and on, if only to give the scientist a bit more "slack" until he thinks up something better. It's when we get into hypothetical realms of this kind that it seems almost beyond science, and we're probably better off going back to just thinking about it all in terms of mystery and wonder. Of course it doesn't help much, and the reader might even be excused for being a bit glazed, when Hawking slips in the odd brain dazzler with what scientists call; "Heisenberg's Uncertainty Principle", which states:

> "it is impossible to know both the exact position and the exact velocity of an object at the same time. However, the effect is tiny and so is only noticeable on a subatomic scale.—By learning the position, you have rendered any information you previously had on the velocity useless. In other words, *the observer affects the observed*". **15**

I think for a lot of us that would stop most conversations dead. And for the next few pages Hawking dips in and out of theories, uncertainties and probabilities to finally remind us of Einstein's question about *God throwing dice before deciding the result of every physical process*. I know Hawking is talking about quantum physics (sub-atomic particles) which is alien to most of us and little to do with our daily buzz. But because his aim is to prove that this is a *new philosophy* that can explain daily events like *soccer balls, turnips and jumbo jets,* I can't see much of it being useful towards a code of living. The point being that any idea of so much *uncertainty* and theory only seems to make any move towards convincing us of the non-existence of God, somewhat fragile – very quickly losing any importance for any new type of "faith" that we might gain from it all. At this point I can just imagine the lads in the pub responding with a little smile, and probably coming up with a few theories of their own, in an attempt to make any relevance sound more "practical", or even entertaining. For example wouldn't it be nice if Heisenberg's idea, that *it is impossible to know both the exact position and the exact velocity of an object at the same time,* worked with speed traps? Then we might have an argument for the photos we get which seem to show both *position* and *velocity* in a flash!

Now professor Hawking's *new philosophy* would really be appealing, but sadly I don't think that's quite what he meant. To be fair, sub-atomic particles in a vacuum are not quite the same thing as a metal box whizzing down the highway.

However when we think about the next statement, *the observer affects the observed,* admittedly meant in a context of quantum physics, we might recognize that it can also be true within an external world of practical living, and therefore does have some relevance. This is nothing new – we only have our sensory perception to go on, and these senses can sometimes fool us. Furthermore we've all experienced *the wish being the father of the thought* – a core within human imagination and a driving force which can promote our wildest dreams. But then this kind of observation should not be the stuff which science is based on, least of all the origin of the universe. Yet we read from Professor McIntosh's research that such a human trait is unavoidable. However as far as origins are concerned and first order questions, *time, velocity* and *position* may be good in the presence of a well-trained human observer, but what if there is no observer? *Will the falling tree in the forest still make a sound if there is no-one to hear it?* – A much debated topic amongst philosophers. Which brings me to the point Dr. Herbert has already mentioned: *No-one was ever around to observe the beginning of the universe* - except God himself; creator and observer, who has made an excellent job of describing it all in Genesis! What better primary evidence of creation is there than that?

Thoughts ---- !

Science can often be blinding to the average reader who may-be desperately trying to apply common sense to it all. leaving him or her positively reeling we might be forgiven for wondering if someone is trying to shift the goal posts a little. And whilst he or she is on the back foot unpacking that one, science can quietly usher God out the back door.

I think slippery use and misuse of any good science either by creative language or otherwise can hardly help its credibility anyway. Surely as far as the man in the street is concerned, who ultimately they're trying to win, he'll probably walk away no wiser. Usually when their nifty theories get caught on the chin, God-bashing debaters often repost with that old favourite; "Well who created God anyway?" - which hopefully puts them back in the contest. After all if God has always existed, why can't some all-powerful creative nothingness have existed as well? Fair comment! But then Heisenberg could flip his own coin when he claims:

"The first gulp from the glass of natural sciences will turn you into an atheist, but at the bottom of the glass God is waiting for you", and for atheism that could be a home goal. **16.**

But if we can skip the bobbing and weaving for a while, in reality, isn't it more like saying if we can't find an answer let's change the rules, blinding us all with the science of the "king's new clothes" which only a few of the "enlightened" might understand ? Prof. Hawking reinforces this quite plainly in ch.3 of *The Grand Design*, especially in p.62 when he seems to make the excuse that our observations are shaped by "a kind of lens, the interpreted structure of our human brains" (in other words our own assumptions as previously discussed) and of course Stephen Hawking does have an excellent brain. So who are we to argue? Having said that I do have to wonder about so called "brainy scientists" when Oxford's professor of chemistry (also a known atheist) Peter Atkins claims that "space-time generates its own dust in the process of its own assembly" **17** He calls this "The Cosmic Bootstrap" principle. In other words you can pull yourself up by your own bootlaces if you want. Or perhaps pick yourself up in a bucket? Not bad for an Oxford prof !

I think with this kind of cosmic dust in the reader's eyes there's little chance of the observer observing anything!

Let's be plain. If Hawking goes on to say that the universe was only waiting for the "blue touch paper to be lit" doesn't common sense ask; what or who put it there in the first place and what or who lit it? Hey! Whose universe is it anyway ?

Philosopher and former atheist, Dr. Anthony Flew makes the point:

"Even if there is only one possible unified theory (e.g. Hawking's theory of everything) it's just a set of rules and equations. What is it that breathes fire into the equations and makes a universe for them to describe"? **18**

As a point of summary so far, I think to rely heavily on science as a reliable tool that could be trusted to give "earthing" to what is an astounding story (and a very human one at that) it might have its shortcomings – especially as a substitute for Divine faith. With pastor Sanderson's miracle and all the supernatural ideas which spin-off, we sometimes find science useful when trying to understand such phenomena and one might expect to get well-balanced points of view and attitudes from such disciplines. But when I hear scientific ideas like a "boot-strap principle" and "something from nothing" my confidence in this kind of "philosophy" plummets and frankly, I am left dazed! And have to honestly ask; now who needs "earthing" ?

Take Hawking's recently published claim that the universe may have created itself, throw in the latest version of that uncertainty magic, giving us a reason to get rid of *cause and effect* (and consequently perhaps even common sense), faith is about the only thing that science has left when trying to deal with the origin of the Universe. The debate has almost fallen back on itself, to which one might add; on this point alone, both sides (science and religion) now stand on equal footing.

Or do they?

The Shakespearean play *Much ado about nothing* depicts so much trickery and falsifications that in the end the whole thing was a fuss about nothing, which indeed they had originally intended to be something. The simplicity of plain truth would have been much wiser. Sounds familiar? I can only conclude that science has some serious limitations, yet has been given such a cathedral of power and authority in our so called enlightened times, that we revere it as the great fount of all knowledge to which we must all bow. And nothing could be further from the truth! On a reality check I don't think William Sanderson would have messed around with word play and fantasies. He was a real man who knew what reality was. When you're as close to the balance between life and death as he was, you can't be doing with fancy "just so stories". I think William Sanderson had his feet well on the ground of reality, or if you like; he was well earthed! The faith he experienced and the faith of the Bible is supernatural and as such conforms to a different set of laws or principles. Minimalists, (those academics who would reduce anything supernatural to nothing more than a pile of chemicals) would have us believe it's all kid-ology or just plain pigheadedness. But ones who embrace it claim otherwise, that it's not earthly but heavenly, not dead but living, neither is it blind but seeing for "Faith is the substance of things hoped for, the evidence of things not (physically) seen". (Heb.11:1).

Jesus said: *Assuredly;"I say to you, whoever does not receive the kingdom of God as a little child will by no means enter it."* Mark 10:15 (New King James Version).

And so to Katy's wisdom

A little girl once said to her mum, "Isn't God great how he made everything just right. I mean just look at my little finger, He made it just the right size to fit up my nose".

How profound and yet so wonderfully innocent and simple was that observation in faith of God's creation. Not far removed from this was a similar statement made centuries earlier by the great Sir Isaac Newton who said

that even "in the absence of any other proof, the thumb alone would convince me of God's existence" **19**. We don't need to be a scientist to apply common sense to the simplicity of what we see. Yet we live in a world that relies on science as a basis of our technological age in which we now live and have our being. However this same science that can accurately put a man on the moon is poor and naked when standing on its own. In a TV interview 2009 professor Winston once said "science is only a version of the truth" **20**. This leads us to conclude there must be other versions: Art, Literature, Music, Language, History, Philosophy and Religion etc. all have a voice and all have an equal status with science. If not then science remains unbridled and ultimately atheistic in attitude, as history as shown through some of the horrors of the past; Hitler, Stalin, Mao, etc. mentioned in ch.6.
Yet to ignore science is not only to tread the path of ignorance and superstition but to throw away a vital tool which in the right hands is a tremendous means of discovering the Creator's handiwork. All evidence needs interpretation and what better guidance for that than the Bible –God's handbook.

We are therefore left with two choices: Either the universe and all life on earth created itself by random chance billions of years ago, or it had a Creator and what we see is evidence of Intelligent Design. There is no middle ground!

Back to the Beginning

Light is the most fundamental and essential ingredient for the creation and development of life. There are many references to it in the Bible as we have already mentioned in chapter 4. In the beginning when God created planet earth He subsequently clothed it in light.

His Light is that *"which gives true light to every man coming into the world"* (John I:9). Natural light is there at birth and supernatural light is there at *new birth*; at salvation. The same light which was there at Creation was there when Jesus rose from the dead and is the same light which wishes to abide in us to make us fit for heaven. (Rom 8:11) So no wonder the Genesis writer saw fit to mention this all important fact of Creation which existed before time itself.

Of course as most sci-fi geeks now know, light and time are related, as Einstein discovered. As most A-level physics students will tell us, it takes about one year for light (in a vacuum) to travel 6 trillion miles, and time is affected by *motion* and *gravity*. For example when an object moves at a speed close to the speed of light, time slows down and at the speed of light it stands still; what physicists call *"time dilation"*. Sounds weird but apparently even a clock at sea level "ticks" slower than one on a mountain, since the clock at sea level is closer to the source of gravity. **21** We could then add on to this wonder of wonders the ideas of different dimensions, parallel universes an' all that which of course make exceedingly good films. But sobering as it may be, Stephen Hawking might just turn down the corners of the chuckle smile a bit when we hear him point out that scientists take some of this stuff quite seriously, especially when they talk in terms of not just three or four dimensions but ten or eleven!

The *truth* is indeed stranger than fiction.

M. Theory

It is generally agreed that the M stands for "membrane", "matrix", or "mother, of all theories", but no one seems to be quite sure. However it does claim it is the nearest thing to *the theory of everything*.

The 11-dimensional M-theory, has to have space and time to have its eleven dimensions, as opposed to the usual three dimensions, (i.e. up-down, forward-back, left-right) plus the fourth dimension of time. During the 1980s a special theory called the string theory was proposed to illustrate this, where the eleventh dimension looks like a small circle or a line. The strings are believed to create vibrations within this multidimensional hyperspace and are thought to correspond to particles that form the basis of everything - all matter and all energy - in existence. Probably a bit like that stringy thing in Star Trek called the "Nemesis" where past, present and future are all contained in one.

An encyclopedia definition states:
"The theory also describes universes like ours, with four observable space-time dimensions, as well as universes with up to 10 flat space dimensions, and also cases where the position in some of the dimensions is not described by a real number, but by a completely different type of mathematical quantity. So the notion of space-time dimension is not fixed in string theory: it is best thought of as different in different circumstances". **22**

As far as Joe Average is concerned this is absolutely incredible and really does shoot us off the planet, if "M theory" is supposed to be a theory of theories with its aim being the theory of everything then that must mean it contains all the laws of the universe and all *other versions of truth* - as everything means everything ! This means at some point we have to allow a *Divine foot* in the door, otherwise it cannot be a science which claims to follow the evidence but instead becomes blinkered and dishonest.

In the Beginning was the Information.

The Laws of the universe which may have, according to Hawking, been there at creation in some kind of vast ocean of nothingness, somehow managed to spark-off the building blocks for the great DNA of total existence. We have aired opinions that laws in themselves cannot create anything. But if we say that the *laws* are not just laws but also information, what then? And if the so called "spontaneous creation" of a universe would require higher "meta", "hyper" or even "super" laws, which may or may not be anything like the laws of physics as we know", then what about that as well? We know that "Hawking cosmology" would like to have us believe that our present universe may have come from another universe and in turn that came from a previous one (multiverse idea) all of which operated in different Laws or "meta/hyper" laws, far removed from anything we know. **23** This is like saying; what would normally be impossible in our universe would be possible in an alien one. And somehow the previous unknown universe gave birth to our known one by just "popping in", lighting *the blue touch paper* and then "popping" back out again. Now if Hawking's "Laws" are information (and I can't see for a second why they are not) then surely we're playing an entirely different ball game .

In his book "In the Beginning was Information", Werner Gitt claims:

"Because information is required for all life processes, it can be stated unequivocally that information is an essential characteristic of all life. All efforts to explain life processes in terms of physics and chemistry will always be unsuccessful. This is the fundamental problem confronting present-day biology, which is based on evolution". (later on in his book he further adds:) "Many scientists therefore justly regard **information** as the third fundamental entity alongside **matter** and **energy**". **24**

Let's accept for a moment that the idea of a *theory of everything,* unifying all ideas and theories into one big package, is a good idea. As Hawking himself suggests it is rather like several see-through overlays on a map which build up the total picture of the landscape which we must study, and because the landmass/subject area is so big this is the only way we can do it to contain or *unify* all the information so that we can know the full picture, or "the mind of God". **25** Now if we want the best picture possible then common sense might suggest that we view all map overlays ever discovered which are valid and have proved themselves operational in the past. Some we may singularly disagree with because it conflicts with the nicety of what we expect the total picture to look like i.e. our world view. So the usual thing to do is to throw it out, as such stuff is "now dead" and has been superseded by the new thing. Unfortunately the layer that we have just thrown out just happens to be a useful version of information which is recognized by a large proportion of mankind and whether you like it or not will just not go away. Theology; the study of the existence of God and Philosophy; the study of cause and the reason for being, have been around from time immemorial and so to throw all that out would clearly be a case of the "observation being affected by the observer" making the whole thing a closed shop! If we want to see the full picture then surely we must embrace all *versions of truth* and that includes the *Divine foot* otherwise we deceive ourselves.

The New Testament letter of St. Paul to Timothy states that in the latter days, prior to the return of Jesus Christ, knowledge (or information) will increase, and seemingly do so on a rapid scale. Nothing could be more correct as we not only worry about the future of the planet but we ironically bathe in a rapidly rising tide of information. This bizarre phenomenon which can be contained and indefinitely stored on tape, discs, and microscopic particles has many versions. Take for example instrumental music, it neither contains words nor pictures yet can feed and inform and even soothe the very soul, and in turn can conjure up some amazing pictures in the mind. It seems to carry no physical mass i.e. weight, nor have any physical shape or colour, yet coveys vast amounts of spiritual energy which can even address some of the most profound philosophical problems in life. This is information. Take art for instance, whether painted or performed in dance it can express the most profound of truths which words alone would fail to do. This is information. And then when we add language and literature to these different expressions their beauty can really soar! What kind of map are we now expecting to see?

The quest for spirituality, either consciously or subconsciously, has always seemed to be at the heart of mankind in his search for fulfilment and a reason for being. To take Hawking's view that within this quantum world of micro, micro, micro particles which make up the very fabric of our being as well as the external universe, the idea that within such a fine-tuned inner fabric of existence is contained multi-dimensions which in some way are connected with other worlds having different physical laws to ours, I wonder if we could be permitted to add some of our own. For example worlds such as heaven and hell have for centuries been preached by the faithful, sometimes to their cost. And what about such dimensions as faith, hope and love. I mean who can explain those for instance without turning to either, art, poetry, music or religion? Furthermore what about miracles? According to Stephen Hawking the concept of *scientific determinism* implies that "there are no miracles or exceptions to the laws of nature." **26** Yet what about the countless miracles which have been claimed by millions throughout the history of civilization, not to mention present day occurrences? Are all these people wrong, mistaken or just lying? No of course not! What about the miracles in the Bible, isn't its whole message based on the miraculous? After all as Werner Gitt claims:

"If God is the Creator of the laws of nature, then He Himself is not subject to them He can use them freely, and can, through His omnipotence, limit their effects or even nullify them" **27**

Even if only a fraction of miracles were found to be 100% true it would be enough to favourably tip the balance. So why can't God just "pop-into" our universe from another world whose laws are different, give us a quick nudge in the right direction, and then "pop-back" out again? And if so why couldn't this have been the process at the beginning of Creation? After all the Hawking model seems to be trying to tell us that the universe seems to have just appeared. Well of course it did! You can't expect a scientist who has an *a priori commitment to materialism*, to be able to see anything else, or to take it any further. **28** He's right. It does just appear to have appeared. Hawking as a pure physicist is only being honest and true to his faith and as such, ironical as it may be, he has done a valuable job which he gets paid for. Some would like to see this as the end of God, but rather it could be more realistically seen as the end of physics, because this is about as good as it gets. At this part in the journey science runs out of steam as Gitt claims:

"All attempts to explain the origin of life by means of models where God as Initiator is ignored, are based on theorem." **29**

And theorem has within it a very large lump of "faith"!

So where's all this getting us?

St Paul writes the famous passage in 1Corinthians,13 that the most important spiritual forces that we can experience in our lives and which are here for our benefit are Faith, Hope and Love. And that the greatest of these is Love! Are not these unfathomable dimensions? Doesn't the Bible deserve some credit? Has it not been shouting this for years? And what about the idea; in the beginning were *laws* or rather *information*? Why does science waste so much time skirting around the issue looking for a single idea which contains the *theory of everything* when the New Testament stares them right in the face when it claims:-

"In the beginning was the Word !" (John 1:1).

The ancient Greeks, prior to and during the time of Jesus, had a high regard for this concept of the all-encompassing "Word" or Logos, a term familiar amongst biblical scholars. To them it was an intangible concept which if ever understood and harnessed was probably the essence of every philosophy and aim in man's attempt to find the *good life.* It was the sum total of what we're all striving for sometimes without knowing it. It was, you might say; *the theory of everything!* **30**

Jesus; Son of Man and Son of God, was the very personification of that Word ! *"Who was with God at the beginning ----- and the Word became flesh and dwelt among us".* (John 1). And not only that but as He (Jesus) was with God in the beginning, and as such knew all things, He was also the Will behind the information which gave it the process, and the sequencing of events for the construction and the pattern of Creation. **31** It is this model or pattern which I believe is the real information. The real Da Vinci code, Holy Grail, Pearl of greatest price, the Logos and the most important thing in life which has to command our attention!

"By faith we understand that the entire universe was formed at God's command, that what we now see did not come from anything that can be seen". (Heb,11:3. NLT)

No conflict

Pastor Sanderson's *star-gate* was no more far-fetched than some of the so-called theories and brainwaves put forward by the great scientific think tanks of our age. In fact if anything the boot is on the other foot which could almost place certain elements of "theoretical science" on the edge of lunacy rather than on the fringe of discovery. If the whole thing comes down to faith, and I'm pretty sure it does, then I'd prefer to put mine in my Creator who lays out practical ideas for living, rather than some academic who's looking to shake us all with his next book. Although to be fair, Hawking cosmology does open up the spiritual dimension, as far as it goes, and is probably closer to the biblical model than we might at first think. For me it enhances my own faith and confirms that; "*The Heavens really do declare the glory of God*" (Ps.19).

In my view the cosmology only goes to show what vast mysteries exist in the universe within the realms of time and space. Newton put it this way:

> "like a boy playing on the sea-shore, and diverting himself in now and then finding a smoother pebble or a prettier shell than ordinary, whilst the great ocean of truth lay all undiscovered before him". **32**

And as such it might cause us to realize that if we dip our toe into the vast ocean of knowledge we could quickly find ourselves out of our depth. True science proves God, and in spite of what may seem like a clumsy groping around in the dark, falling short by trying to keep the *Divine foot out the door*, Stephen Hawking, in his own unique way treads a spiritual path common to us all. Except for that very thin line between atheism and theism, I think that Hawking and Sanderson would have got on very well had they been around at the same time. Would they have discussed the *theory of everything*? Maybe so, but somehow I think I might faintly hear William saying, "theory, equation? Oh no, it's more than that! - It's the Answer!"

Conclusion

Cosmology goes to show how the vast mysteries of the universe cannot be explained by science alone in the absence of God and therefore falls short. Religion and philosophy are tools by which it can be taken further.

Stephen Hawking and William Sanderson are both men of faith. One finds faith in theoretical science, the other in Divine experience.

A theory of everything is of little use unless it embraces all versions of truth and is relevant to practical every-day living.

The "Logos" ("Word") is also identified as a "theory" of everything and is personified in Jesus Christ.

References

1. Professor Richard Lewontin Leading geneticist. "Delusion of Evolution". (Nottingham: New Life Publication)-4th edition.
A priori meaning hypothetical conclusion based on deduction .

2. Acts of the Apostles is an excellent historic record of some of the pitfalls and triumphs of the early church.

3. Occam's Razor. William of Ockham (*c*. 1285–1349) is remembered as an influential nominalist though his popular fame as a great logician rests chiefly on the maxim attributed to him and known as Ockham's razor. It is a principle urging one to select from among competing hypotheses that which makes the fewest assumptions. ----Wikipedea. 2013

4. Stephen Hawking. "The Grand Design" (London: Bantam Books, 2010), p13.

5. John Lennox. "God and Stephen Hawking" p.18.

6. Richard Dawkins interview with John Mackay: "The Genius of Charles Darwin: Richard Dawkins, Channel 4 (UK), Monday 18th August 2008.

7. Stephen Hawking. "The Grand design" p132 – 133.

8. Stephen Hawking. "A Brief History of Time" (London: Bantam Books, 1988), p 193

9. Ibid. p187

10. Stephen Hawking. “The Grand design” p227.

11. John Lennox: Professor of Mathematics and the Philosophy of Science, Oxford University. “God and Stephen Hawking” (Oxford: Lion Books. 2010), p.16.

12. Dr. Jake Hebert is Research Associate at the Institute for Creation Research. Cited; creationministries.com

13. John Lennox. “God and Stephen Hawking” p.30

14. Dr Andy McIntosh, Genesis for today” (Day One publications. 2001). P14.

15. http://www.h2g2.com/Math Science &Technology > Physics Created Jun 10, 2003 | Updated Nov 22, 2011

Werner:-Heisenberg-Quotes. Http://www..goodreads.com/author/quoses/64309.Werner-Heisen --- 04/07/2013.

Also p.62 in “The Grand design” suggests how our brain’s interpretation has a great influence on our conclusions.

16 Ibid . Http://www..goodreads.com/author/quoses/64309.Werner-Heisen, 2013

17. “Creation Revisited.” Penguin 1994.p143 Peter Atkins cited in “God and Stephen Hawking” p.31

18. Antony Flew. "There is a God" (New York, Harper, 2007), p.97. How the world's most notorious atheist changed his mind.

19 refspace.com -- Isaac Newton quotes.

20. Interview with Professor Winston "Room 101" TV chat-show. 2009 .

21. Dr John Hartnett: Physicist and Meteorlogical research scientist; University of Western Australia. " Starlight Time and the New Physics". Ch.2. Ref. also; Wikki encyclopaedia.

22. String theory From Wikipedia, the "Free Encyclopaedia".

23. Stephen Hawking. "The Grand design" pp.174 .

24. Werner Gitt. "In the Beginning Was Information". (Stuttgart: CLV Publications. 2000), pp,9 &44.

25. Hawking: "The Grand Design" p,17

26. Ibid. p,48

27. Gitt. " In the Beginning was Information" p,34,

28. See reference 1.

29. Gitt. "In the Beginning was Information" p 33

30. Logos.

"Greek: "word," "reason," or "plan", plural logoi, in Greek philosophy and theology, the divine reason implicit in the cosmos, ordering it and giving it form and meaning. Though the concept defined by the term logos is found in Greek, Indian, Egyptian, and Persian philosophical and theological systems, it became particularly significant in Christian writings and doctrines to describe or define the role of Jesus Christ as the principle of God active in the creation and the continuous structuring of the cosmos and in revealing the divine plan of salvation to man. It thus underlies the basic Christian doctrine of the pre-existence of Jesus.- Encyclopedia Britannica

31. Werner Gitt. chapter 3 "In the Beginning was information"

32. *Memoirs of the Life, Writings, and Discoveries of Sir Isaac Newton* (1855) by Sir David Brewster (Volume II. Ch. 27). Compare: "As children gath'ring pebbles on the shore".

Chapter 8.
Patterns ---- and Blackberries.

Earth's crammed with heaven,

And every common bush
afire with God;
But only he who sees,
takes off his shoes,
The rest sit round it
and pluck blackberries,
And daub their
natural faces unaware.–

Elizabeth Browning. -- 1

It's not difficult to recognize pattern and order that exists within our universe. All of us are deeply aware now, especially with constant reminders of the need for global conservation, that nature is indeed finely tuned and balanced but so easily damaged. Scientists often refer to this fine tuning as the "Goldilocks effect" because it's just right, meaning that it is so finely tuned that it *appears* to have been made solely for our purpose.2 Well that's because it has! Even some of the more agnostic amongst the science fraternity reluctantly have to admit that nature has the *appearance* of design. Well that's because it is, *designed* ! Stephen Hawking in his book "*The Grand Design*" suggests that a good model, (idea or theory for the origin of the universe) must be "elegant".3

Well the idea of Creation having a Creator is, *elegant!*

Science can sound terribly rude sometimes when it attempts to reduce Creation to a pile of mathematical junk, and then has the arrogance to call it *appearance of beauty*. The cosmos and all that is in it, has the appearance of beauty because it is indeed beautiful. To the beholder yet it may be, but then that's why we are here - to behold! The garden is only complete with the gardener, or the canvas with the artist, and so on. We have within us a spiritual capacity which makes us unique in the animal kingdom which has come about because we are made in God's image, giving us our *raison d'etre!* In the previous chapter we spoke about the importance of Heaven needing to be "earthed", and how the concept of the *Logos* is that point of connection. In this chapter I hope to give a few examples of how its presence might be visible and relevant.

Don't miss the point

In the Genesis story of Adam and Eve we find a beautiful picture of paradise. Although later sadly lost, it was the pattern which God had in mind for us all as His intention was for mankind to live in harmony with all Creation including God Himself. This is probably why we are creatures of habit, which tends to sound a little mundane and negative. Perhaps what we mean to say is that we like familiar routine or style of living, in other words some sort of meaningful creative pattern with sense and purpose; happiness being the ultimate aim. I'm sure that most of us will agree that our main aim during our time on earth is happiness and fulfilment. This I'm sure is why we express our skills in creativity or look forward to things like holidays, retirement, or a new something or other which we believe will answer the yearning within. Many of the great religions of the world have deeply studied this. Take Buddhism for example; its main philosophy for happiness is based on simplicity of life, meditation, harmony and ultimate enlightenment. We all strive for our own Eden which I believe we innately recognise as a paradise lost which must somehow be regained; beautiful gardens, landscapes, peace and quiet or even just messing about in boats in a shady river creek whilst being wafted along by an evening summer breeze. And as we drift along perhaps we might just catch a glimpse of some of the wonderful patterns that there are in nature. How flowers, animals, birds and even the spider's web carry a small cosmic resemblance to that Great Order. Their symmetry carries a mathematical signature of the Creator of all patterns who is the "God of order, not chaos".

There's little wonder that William Blake became inspired by that blazing sight when he wrote:

TIGER, tiger, burning bright
In the forests of the night,
What immortal hand or eye
Could frame thy fearful
symmetry?

What an elegant sight and yet what a powerful masterpiece of engineering!

When the stars threw down their spears,
And water'd heaven with their tears,
Did He smile His work to see?---

--Did He who made the lamb make thee? -4

Yes of course He did but it's so easy to miss it .
Isn't it ?

I'm sure that Elizabeth Browning's intention was to drive home this all too important point when she wrote that; "*only he who sees takes of his shoes*" whilst the rest just "*pick blackberries and daub their faces*".
It is this seeing, or eye of faith as it were, that makes all the difference.
Can you remember those illusory patterns that give a different picture when viewed from different angles? Well it's the same with our perception of the world around us; it all depends on our world-view. Or if you like the glasses we wear. If we see creation as nothing more than a pile of atoms from which we can selfishly exploit and gain our fill then that's about as good as it gets, and *you have your reward.* Yes blackberries taste great and God indeed gave us the fruit of the vine to eat and enjoy, even sell and pay due taxes. But when we've "rendered unto Caesar that which is Caesar's" don't forget to "render unto God that which is God's". In other words get the balance right. Feed the belly for sure but don't neglect the soul. Give credit where it's due because:-

"Earth's crammed with heaven,
And every common bush afire with God;
But only he who sees, takes off his shoes".

The pattern has no limit

Some years ago I owned a 350cc Royal Enfield motorcycle. A single cylinder classic machine, beautifully soft tuned, sweet little power unit that took me to work daily across some of the most beautiful and often bleak parts of the Derbyshire Peak District. Its design had long been surpassed by many of those plastic rockets we see today which silently whistle down the road divorced from their ancestral throaty sounds, reminiscent of a bygone age. Locked in time her long stroke piston "tonked" as she meandered through leafy country lanes, whilst her large seven inch headlamp pierced its leading beam through the moist droplets of a half lit morning mist. Man and Machine..."Tonktonktonk," went the rhythm ... same pace ... no longer anything to prove... did that years ago... learnt more sense. Up-hill, down-dale, and yet up again. Same pace ... "Don't change gear yet, leave it to me, trust me"... "Tonktonk," went her heartbeat. Not too fast nor too slow, time to look, sniff the air as man on chrome ascends to greet dawn's golden haze. Ah, life's good! This is the pace, this is the pattern, almost music... "Tonk,tonk,tonk"!

When I reflect back on those days I can't fail to recognise the Divine pattern yet again. Why confine it to nature alone? Isn't this human connection part of it as well even if it takes an oily, man- made machine to help us connect? Yet just another tool to help paint that Divine Word on the canvas of the heart.

Our self-sufficiency and science often causes us to boast and take credit for such achievements when the reality of it all is that we can do nothing without creation's power and permission. How aptly put is the hymn:

God of concrete , God of steel, God of piston and of wheel.

God of pylon God of steam, God of girder and of beam.

God of atom, God of mine. All the world of power is thine! **-5**

In his book, *The God Who Speaks* Benedictine monk Ian Petit, admitted that for years he failed to make the connection between the God he experienced in nature and the God he was supposed to see in the church. He writes that it was eventually through the enlightenment of the Holy Spirit that the scales fell from his eyes and the penny dropped. **6** Our sighting of God's hand is never limited to nature's flora and fauna alone. He will and does manifest his charm throughout all aspects of human experience; even in the whizzing and popping of wheels, chains and gears. "And no idea that you have of God *is* God.

We are tempted to wrap him up in definitions, tie Him down to our human concepts, box him up in our doctrines. How right it is that God should forever burst out of these confines, shatter our images and make us realise He is greater than our wildest thoughts."**7**

It was yet another monk, this time a 17th century Carmelite, Brother Lawrence who trained himself to do everything for the love of God, even in the chaos of the kitchen where he worked 15 years and where he would normally have had a strong natural aversion. He had learned a pattern which gained him great rewards. He called it "practising the presence of God". Meaning that the time of prayer was in no way different from any other. **8**

It is through this wider vision of God's presence that we are invited to join in and connect. It's a gift for the taking; all we have to do is accept it. Jesus - master of the art of living, Lord of Creation, omnipresent in every particle of every fabric of the universe and beyond - personified a unique and simple pattern for life. He is the pattern which is so "finely tuned for our existence", that if we're not grafted in it, and He in us, then we're missing out! We are meant to be part of it.

Jesus said "The kingdom of Heaven is within you" (Luke 17:21). And how true it is because this is where our journey begins and ends, within the very core. Ultimately we are responsible for our own response to the Gift. God gives us free will and choice and He will not barge in or interfere with those who don't want to know. It is for this reason that Jesus profoundly emphasised that for some

"---their heart has become calloused; they hardly hear with their ears, and they have closed their eyes. Otherwise they might see with their eyes, hear with their ears, understand with their hearts and turn, and I would heal them."(Matt.13:13-15).

In other words ignorance of the Gift may be blissfully excusable but to knowingly turn it aside is not.

Sadly this is the state of the human heart, although "light has come into the world, men loved darkness rather than light because their deeds were evil."(John 3:19).

Is there any wonder the world is in such a mess?

How blind we must be not to recognise pattern etched on every part of the fabric and in every vibration of life that *even the stones cry out*. (Luke 19:40)

> Or: *Split a piece of wood and God is there,*
> *Lift a stone and you will find God."*---
> Gospel of Thomas–**9**

The Golden Ratio.

During the 1850s Adolf Zeising, a German psychologist who was interested in mathematics and philosophy, recognised what seemed to be a universal pattern predominant in all nature. The Golden Ratio as it is termed was believed to have been existent in the minds of the ancient Greeks and Egyptians and was a general observation in their applications of mathematics and design. Zeising noticed that this golden ratio not only expressed itself within the structures of plants and veins in leaves but was also present in the anatomy of humans and animals even to the tree-like pattern of veins, nerves and sinews etc. Recognising that this was also present throughout Creation he went on to identify it in all aspects of science and art. In 1854 Zeising wrote of a universal law:

10

"in which is contained the ground-principle of all formative striving for beauty and completeness in the realms of both nature and art, and which permeates, as a paramount spiritual ideal, all structures, forms and proportions, whether cosmic or individual, organic or inorganic, acoustic or optical; which finds its fullest realization, however, in the human form." **-11**

The Golden ratio is basically a mathematical term that describes a ratio of 1 to 1.618 that is commonly found in nature. Looking at it visually it we get an idea of the relative proportions seen in the flower diagram, (a-b). Because it is pleasing to the eye, many artists used it to plan their paintings. Leonardo DaVinci was probably the most famous artist to use the Golden Ratio in his work.

God is a creator of order, and what better way is there for Him to reveal such than through patterns.

When applying this principle to just about everything whether art, science, literature or music etc. even the Ten Commandments (Decalogue – meaning "ten words") is not far removed from this ratio.

This heart of the Jewish Torah (meaning instruction) was, and still is, deemed to contain a vital pattern for life. Divided into two parts the Decalogue contains the first four laws concerning man's relationship with God and the remaining six concerning man's relationship with his fellow man.

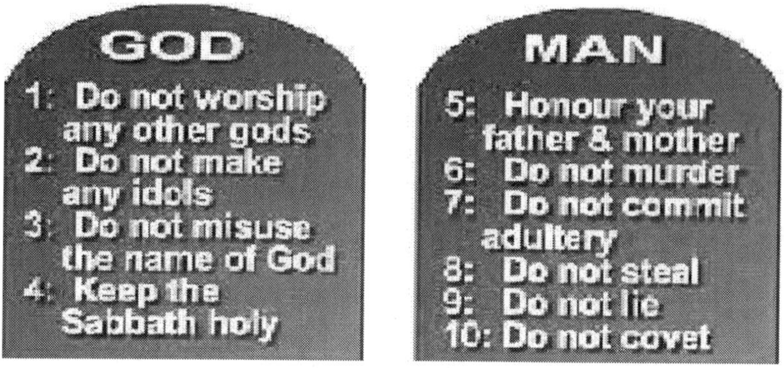

GOD
1: Do not worship any other gods
2: Do not make any idols
3: Do not misuse the name of God
4: Keep the Sabbath holy
MAN
5: Honour your father & mother
6: Do not murder
7: Do not commit adultery
8: Do not steal
9: Do not lie
10: Do not covet

Notice that the initial observation of the Decalogue gives us a ratio of 4 to 6 i e 1 to1.5.

However when we consider that Commandment No. 4 is shared between both respect for God and concern for man's welfare the two parts of the commandments become even closer to the golden ratio; possibly between our initial 1.5 and say 1.8 - averaging out somewhere nearer our golden number of 1.61 etc. **12**

Although this may seem to be scientifically packaging what is essentially spiritual, what remains is something which is vital for quality of life.

"My way is easy" -- Jesus

What emerges from this is what Jesus had to say about it. Much of what He said often referred to the Jewish Law (Commandments), as this was the heart of their way of life ordained by God. Recognising that many of the so called religious people of the day strictly muscled their way through this "keeping of the Law" by sheer grit and determination, and even then failed to keep it all, Jesus simplified the pattern with little more than two words: *Love God and love your neighbour* (Mark 12:30-31), something which is often referred to in theology as the *Golden Rule*.

When we look at the Decalogue we can see how its two parts can be summarised accordingly under such two headings - e g, *respect for God and respect for man.* The way it works is this: If you genuinely love God, the natural trade-off from this has the power to produce concern for the welfare of your fellow man, meaning enemies as well as friends. So if you love God, you'll love people (Matt.5:43-45). In other words the two parts of the Ten Commandments are designed to complement each other and to automatically take place with minimum of effort making the lifestyle natural, or should we say *supernatural,* in the sense that this is how God intended our *natural* lives to be. This was not a means by which one could abandon the demand of the law- an easy alternative - but a higher way of upholding the standard of the law as it is now written in the heart. This balance of lifestyle is indeed a *golden ratio* because it is a *living thing* within the innermost being, and no-longer needs to be carved in stone. What the Law could not do, Jesus made possible (Rom.8). Of course something like this still requires vigilance and commitment. Even St Paul commented on the constant need to maintain *Christ's rule of peace within* as a guiding light. Not forgetting:

"It is for freedom that Christ has set us free; stand firm then, and do not let yourself be burdened again by a yoke of slavery" (Galatians 5:1).NIV.

The biblical phrase being "born again" just about sums it up - (John 3:6-8). Not in the natural sense but by the power of the Holy Spirit ... "to be renewed in the spirit of your mind", (Eph. 4:23). St Paul summed it up like this:

"I am crucified with Christ: nevertheless I live; yet not I, but Christ lives in me: and the life which I now live in the flesh I live by the faith of the Son of God, who loved me, and gave himself for me".(Gal. 2:20).

Therefore to be born of the Spirit means that Jesus becomes the source of our righteousness, not us.

In this chapter I have tried to use several examples to show the importance of patterns, not just as an unavoidable part of nature but as a universal signature of God's power and intelligent design. The concept of patterns seems to be mechanism itself, bristling with order and purpose and whether we like it or not we are part of it. The "Jesus Pattern"- the *Logos* is the human connection, which is not just a fulfilment of Divine Law but ... "The way the Truth and the Life." - (John 14:6)

William Sanderson's life style was one which followed this pattern devotedly, resulting in great blessings through the relationship he had with his Creator. He was a man who demonstrated how such a relationship is indeed possible, and for him the *star-gate* which although was once inaccessible through Adam was now accessible through Christ. He was a humble man who lived a simple life yet whose richness in spiritual and moral values is one to be admired and much sought after in today's fast living world. In the next and final chapters, I wish to show how this Divine pattern is not only meant to be our personal destiny, but a way of salvation for humanity as a whole.

Conclusion

The principle of patterns exists throughout all aspects of Creation and shows powerful evidence for intelligent design.

Its beauty, purpose and relevance permeate into every aspect of life as a spiritual ideal which seeks fulfilment in the completeness of human experience. This is the Logos – the "Living Word".

Only through recognition of the Divine can a transformation take place within, enabling us to access the source of all life and thereby find our true identity as God intended.

Notes and references

1. Elizabeth Browning; (1806 – 61). British writer, Elizabeth Barrett Browning was a Romantic poet, and wife of Robert Browning. Extract taken from her poem/novel; "Aurora Leigh". 1856.

2.Stephen Hawking "A Brief History of Time" – (London:Bantam Books. 1988), p.139.

3. Stephen Hawking. " The Grand Design" (London: Bantam Books . 2010), p,68

4. William Blake. "The Tiger" – "Oxford Book of English Verse: 1250 – 1900"

5. Richard G Jones. "God of concrete God of steel---" Words copyright 1969 by Galliard Ltd.

6. Ian Petit.OSB." The God Who Speaks",(London: Daybreak Publications, 1989), pp74 – 75.

7. Ibid.

8. E.M.Blaiklock. "The Practice of the Presence of God".(London: Hodder & Stoughton. 1981) P24. Translation of the works of 17th century French monk, Brother Lawrence.

9. The Gospel of Thomas. Non-canonical, early church (1st&2nd century) references to the life and teachings of Jesus. Discovered near Nag Hammadi, Egypt, in December 1945. It is one of a group of books which are associated with the early Gnostic writings some of

which are considered suspect by certain scholars. The particular reference to "The Gospel of Thomas" used here is cited in the film;"Stigmata"-1999.

10.Adolf Zeising.1810 -76 The Golden Ratio. – Wikipedia, free encyclopedia – internet. 2013

11. Ibid.

12. *"Remember the Sabbath day, to keep it holy.*[9] *Six days you shall labour and do all your work,* [10] *but the seventh day is the Sabbath of the LORD your God. In it you shall do no work: you, nor your son, nor your daughter, nor your male servant, nor your female servant, nor your cattle, nor your stranger who is within your gates----"*. Exodus 20:8-11 (NKJV)

Although Commandment No.4 initially states that the Sabbath is to be kept holy thereby showing man's respect for God, a large proportion of it offers advice on the community benefits gained by properly taking care of human requirements. Because therefore it is shared - (proportions being unknown) - between man's respect for both God and fellow man- practicalities of a Sabbath day structure would have flexibilities according to social and spiritual needs.

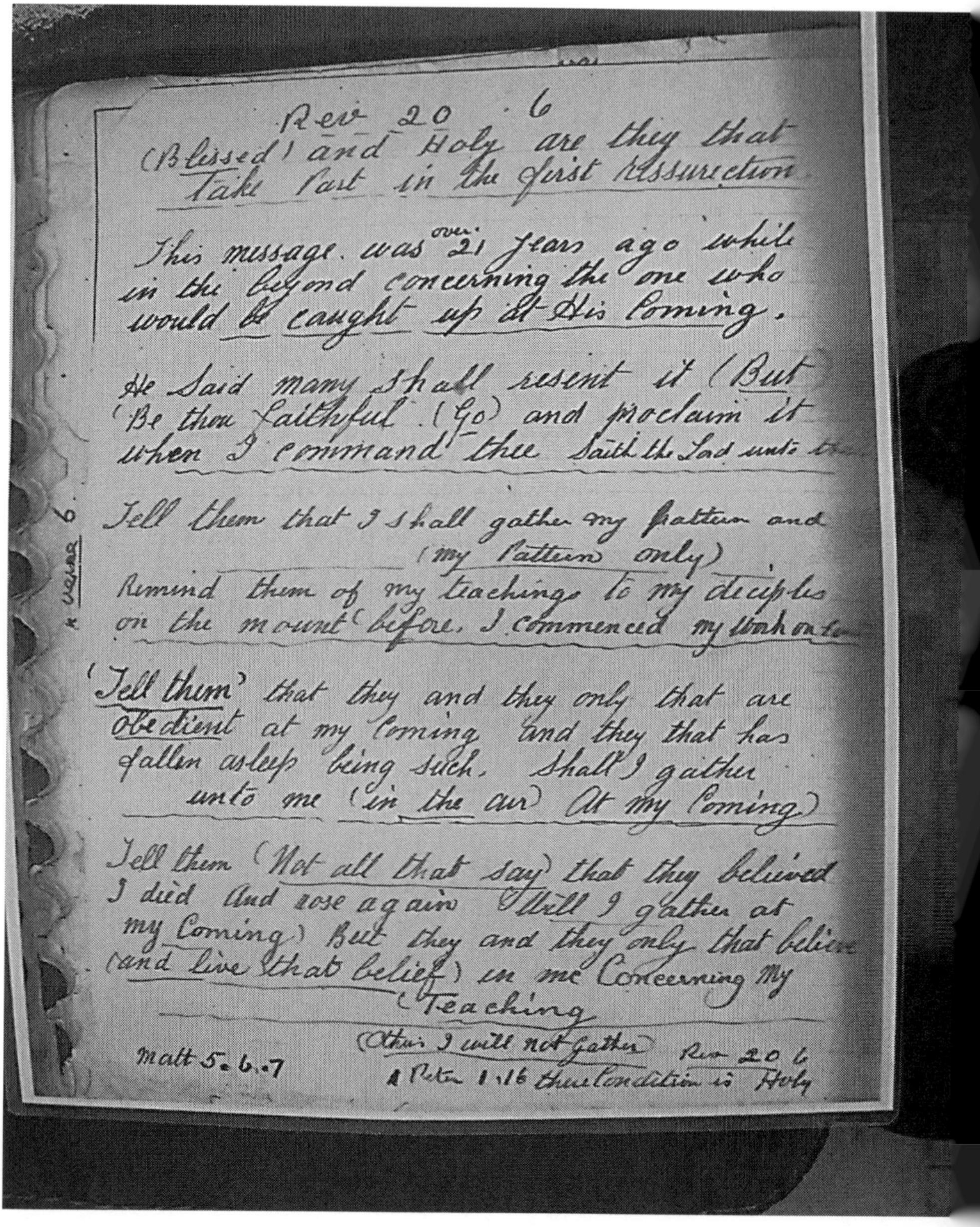

Rev 20 . 6
(Blessed) and Holy are they that
Take Part in the first Ressurection

This message was over 21 years ago while
in the beyond concerning the one who
would be caught up at His Coming.

He Said many shall resent it (But
'Be thou faithful' (Go) and proclaim it
when I command thee Saith the Lord unto th[ee]

verse 6.

Tell them that I shall gather my pattern and
(my Pattern only)
Remind them of my teachings to my deciples
on the mount before I commenced my Work on ea[rth]

'Tell them' that they and they only that are
Obedient at my Coming and they that has
fallen asleep being such. Shall I gather
unto me (in the air) At my Coming)

Tell them (Not all that say) that they believed
I died And rose again Will I gather at
my Coming) But they and they only that believe
(and live that belief) in me Concerning My
(Teaching

(Others I will not gather) Rev 20 6
Matt 5.6.7 1 Peter 1.16 their Condition is Holy

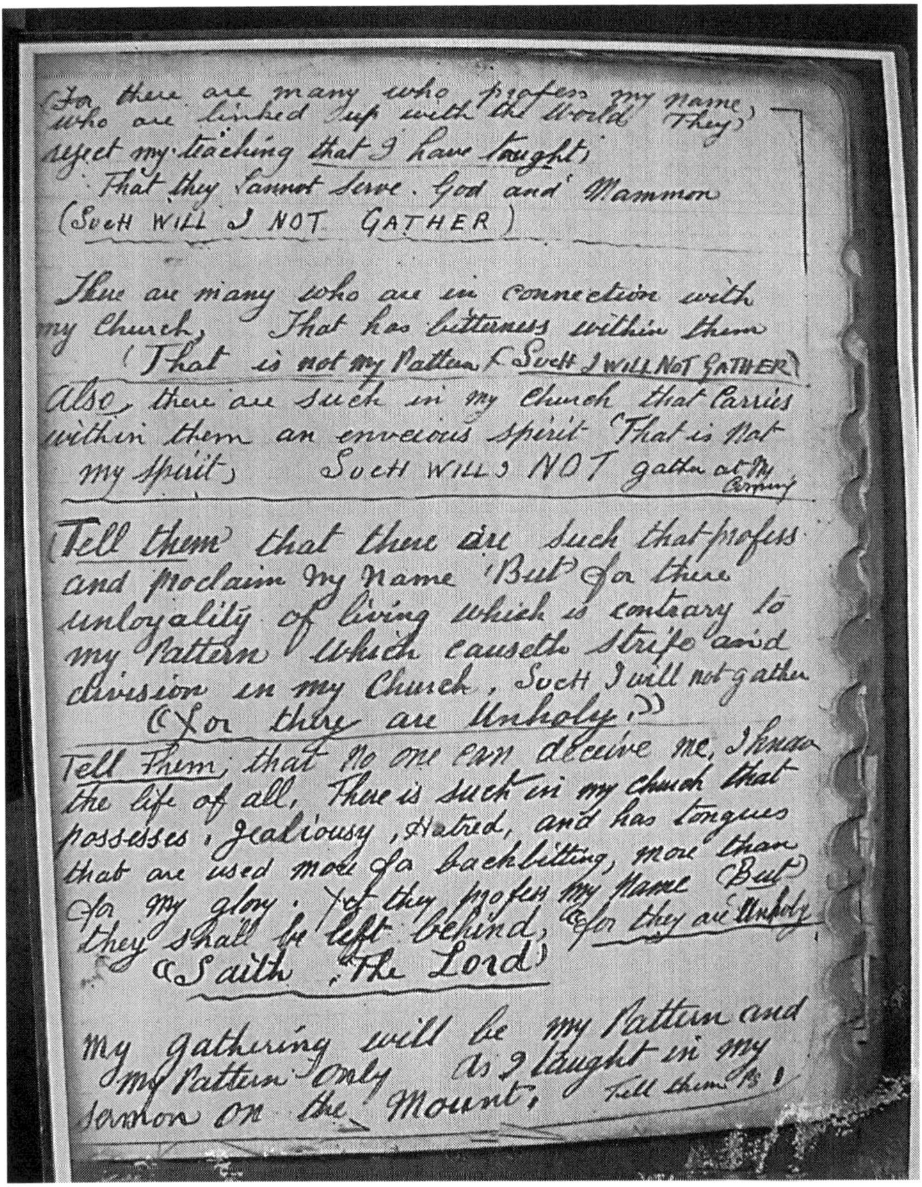

(For there are many who profess my name
who are linked up with the World (They)
reject my teaching that I have taught,
That they cannot Serve. God and Mammon
(SUCH WILL I NOT GATHER)

There are many who are in connection with
my Church, That has bitterness within them
(That is not my Pattern (SUCH I WILL NOT GATHER)
Also, there are such in my Church that Carries
within them an envious Spirit 'That is Not
my Spirit) SUCH WILL I NOT gather at My
Company

(Tell them that there are such that profess
and proclaim My Name 'But' for there
unloyality of living which is contrary to
my Pattern which causeth Strife and
division in my Church, SUCH I will not gather
("For they are Unholy.")
Tell Them, that No one can deceive me, I know
the life of all, There is such in my church that
possesses, jealiousy, Hatred, and has tongues
that are used more for backbiting, more than
for my glory. For they profess my Name (But)
they shall be left behind, (for they are Unholy
("Saith, The Lord")

My gathering will be my Pattern and
my Pattern Only As I taught in my
Sermon On the Mount, Tell them Ps.

Pastor Sanderson's Bible showing his hand written message which was to form his sermon notes.

– previous page.

Chapter 9 The Message.

Let's open Pastor Sanderson's book, or rather his Bible.(previous page) It's hard to describe, the emotions I felt when I first held what I consider to be an awesome relic of the past, yet an object as up to date in its content as ever. Feeling through the well-used pages one couldn't help sense that here was a true instrument of the pulpit. This was an icon of the days gone by and one could almost hear the thunderous heartfelt roar of that old gospel message sounding out into the congregation. Immediately I was aware of the well-worn pages and added notes written and dotted in and around the corners as was the usual custom amongst many preachers of the gospel, and still is today.

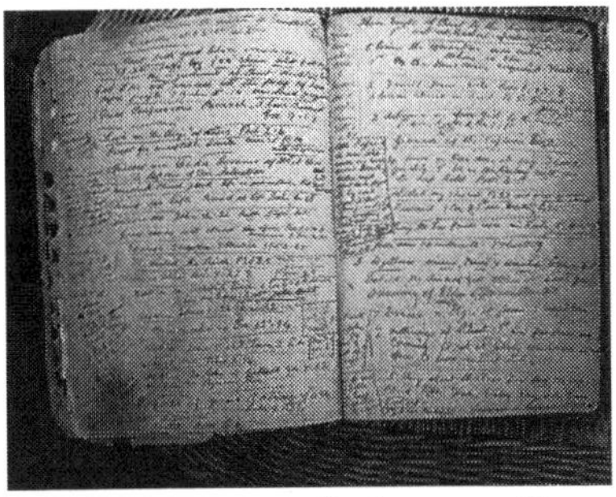

Fingers meandering about two thirds through suddenly find two additional large lined sheets on which is written William's message given to him by Jesus "whilst in the beyond". Well glued in situ, this was obviously meant to be further annotated material and the centre of his many sermons from the pulpit. This of course was his testimony, and his best and maybe his only profound sermon; now his life's mission.

Containing mainly direct speech the instructions are clear and precise and do not mince words. The layout seems similar to that of any preacher's or lecturer's notes used to steer passage through a sermon or lesson. The use of two ink penned colours (red & black) would be to prevent eye wandering and to help the speaker focus on the sequencing of the script, similar to how we might use computer graphics and coloured fonts today in order to mark, round off and open up points we wish to make.
The opening lines of the message are immediate and profound. No beating around the bush here. It makes a non-compromising point that the standard is high and eventual judgement is inevitable.

This is not a wishy-washy gospel neither does it give two hoots about giving offence but is more concerned about man's eternal destiny as opposed to his temporal comfort. Its clear message is a reprimand aimed primarily at hypocrisy in the church, but then the spin-off shows that none of us can dodge this one either.

The message opens up with the book of Revelation chapter 20, which basically states:
1. Christ will come to earth again but this time in majestic judgement.
2. Holiness is His pattern and His pattern alone!

The Message

Although these are basically laid out as sermon notes they contain, as believed by William direct first hand instructions from Jesus.

I have attempted to picture myself standing in the pulpit about to deliver a similar sermon from these notes to a modern day congregation. I am not going to attempt a neat three point sermon as is the custom amongst the skilled, but simply aim to deliver it as it is, warts an' all. The message is profound and sincere and is rather heavy in the landing. It doesn't need any modern audio/ visual aids because our imagination should be enough to hold the attention. Far from trying to put myself in the same league as William Sanderson the following literary "depiction" of his sermon content is meant only to be used as a device, hoping to expound certain points relevant to a 21st century church and is completely subject to my own interpretation:-

And so to preach.

Good morning church !

My sermon today will be based on the notes of Pastor William Sanderson as I believe he may have wished it to be delivered:

Revelation.Ch20:6.
"Blessed and Holy are they that take part in the first resurrection."

Facing the Star-gate

The text is plain. If you want to get into Heaven make sure you're amongst this crowd. Because when we read on, the ones who follow aint gonna be so lucky! Fearsome as it appears to read I just don't want to be around for the second house, nor would I wish it for anyone else for that matter.

Now, reading the context of Revelation 20, it gives us a picture of a zero tolerance judgement.

There's no slick lawyer here to fight your corner, no human rights activist to get you a sympathy vote, you're on your own, and claiming "oops" just isn't an option!

So it's no good saying, "Oh I'll wait and see but for now I'll leave all that Jesus stuff an' see what happens when the time comes or something. *Now is the time says the Lord* ! (Isaiah 1:18). That is unless your name is written in the Book of Life, anyone not found in this one "is cast into the lake of fire". (Rev.20:15.

And this is where it gets heavy!

Now I know this all sounds a bit severe but in the end the Big Boss has all the cards and none of us down here can tweak the rules one iota. Shooting the messenger and ranting at the message won't make the slightest bit of difference as your name's either in or not in, and that is the crux of the matter.

The gospel is not soft as many would see it. This is no middle class tea-on-the-lawn chat with the vicar and a few nice little old ladies, but a take it on the chin challenge.

And:

The Message

"many shall resent it But be thou faithful Go and proclaim it--------"

No atheistic no-god "let's face the hard truth" cop-out here, 'cos if you want the hard truth this is worse. Any so-called oblivion based on a cowardly atheistic and suicidal easy-way-out philosophy suddenly pales at the side of this one. No, this is hot and strong, and non-belief or belief in any alternative won't make the slightest bit of difference.

You know there's no wonder that many Christians in the past have been grossly unpopular when delivering this message. But then a message like this has often proved to have been beneficial to society in the end.
Take the Wesleyan revival for example during the 18th century. Historian W E H Lecky claimed: that if it hadn't been for this, Britain may have been plunged into revolution like the French. 1 Yet the pioneers of this searing message, in the face of much moral decline, were met with heated opposition, hatred and even violent abuse during the early days. But like an unpalatable medicine, it rendered beneficial healing to the nation and a great boost to morale with restoration of both personal and national respect. However like all good things it came at a price, and somebody at some point had to make him or herself pretty unpopular.

'A.G. Gardener wrote: *"The prophet is only useful so long as he is stoned as a public nuisance, calling us to repentance, disturbing our comfortable routines, breaking our respectable idols and shattering our sacred conventions.'* **2**. ----- And a message like this is indeed prophetic!

So it's really about personal accountability. It's certainly not escapism, a criticism some would throw at Christianity. It's all about our personal responsibility to both *Man & God*. For some the man bit might be easy and may even give us some sort of self-atoning feeling of pride in a "doing-our-bit" buzz, especially when in receipt of the odd "Jack Horner" award and public limelight- you know: "what a good boy am I". It's the God bit that's the real challenge. The 'oo well I don't want to get too bogged down with that one stance. Or the classic "Now I'm not religious" (as if those who are have the plague or something) "and I'm not a church goer but---". And they usually go on to give some highly moral and less cringy opinion on how somebody ought to save the starving millions, deal with the bad guys, sort the economy; finally blaming the Government, which is usually a good common target on which we can all vent our frustrations. Well that's fine for the now, but what about our eternal destiny? In case we haven't noticed we're not going to be here for too long, and some less long than others. And no matter how many "atoning" Brownie points we can clock up hoping to soften up the Ol' Man in the sky when our time comes, and no matter how much religious or non-religious self-righteousness we can brag about, I hate to knock your duck off but, it just won't work. Why? Because it's just not good enough -----Aggh! What !!! After all I've done !

Yep! 'fraid so : . *"For I tell you that unless your righteousness surpasses that of the Pharisees and the teachers of the law, you will certainly not enter the kingdom of Heaven"*, (Matt. 5:20) NIV.

---- And there was nobody more goody-goody than them.

Still not convinced ?

OK what about someone who does some outstanding charitable work and maybe raises millions of pounds and dollars to help the less fortunate. They may have devoted most of their life to others and been held in high esteem by all, but sadly one day fate takes a hand and through either temptation or misfortune they commit a terrible crime for which the penalty is a jail sentence. Now when standing before the judge, no matter how much good works can be used in defence, doesn't the fact remain that because the law has been broken punishment must be given ? Get the point ?

So it's not so much about being good but about being made good enough, and that can only happen through the atoning sacrifice that Jesus made for us on our behalf on the cross. The penalty was paid once and for all. This is the gift of God's Grace, all we have to do is recognise our need and accept it. But then our part is to live it by transmitting some of the grace we have received to others. And that starts in the heart! Freely you've received - freely give.

Mother Teresa once said:
“It's not about how much you do, but how much love you put into what you do that counts." - (1910-1997) **3.**

Often referred to by Jesus as whitewashed tombs, the hypocrisy of certain Pharisees and teachers of the law was compared to someone who only cleaned their pots and pans on the outside for all to see whilst their inner lives were in tatters. Yet their strict ascetic religiosity in keeping the letter of the Law, (whilst at the same time wielding the hard stick of legalism on the “weaker brethren”) was second to none. But their hearts were hard, a faint reminder of how God Himself refused Cain’s gift, right at the beginning of the Bible, because it was not given with a good heart.
Can you see the church here somewhere in this? God forbid that she falls into this kind of hypocrisy ! Such is not the Jesus pattern.

It’s not about the art of good works, but about God’s works of the heart.
Here’s what St Paul had to say about it in 1.Corinthians 13:1-3 :

“If I speak in the tongues of men or of angels, but do not have love, I am only a resounding gong or a clanging cymbal. If I have the gift of prophecy and can fathom all mysteries and all knowledge, and if I have a faith that can move mountains, but do not have love, I am nothing. If I give all I possess to the poor and give over my body to hardship that I may boast, but do not have love, I gain nothing” --NIV.

The Message

***"Tell them that I shall gather my pattern and my pattern only
Remind them of my teaching to my disciples on the Mount before I commenced my work on earth"***

The Sermon on the Mount was radical. Considered the greatest sermon ever preached it contains the essential pattern for our lives. (Matthew 5-7) There's no government health warning here. Words like, *if your eye causes you to sin pull it out, or your hand cut it off!* Shock statements were common place even in those days. Attention it would certainly draw especially from someone who has just been healing the sick, and now talks of dismembering yourself! No the aim here is not so much the action but what really lies behind it. "Even if a man so much as looks at a woman lustfully he has already committed adultery with her in his heart". You know fellas that leering look? Or, If a man hates his fellow man he is guilty of murder. Purity of heart is so important that we ought to be saying; "I'd give my right arm for it!" Get the point? This is the Jesus pattern; where we spend eternity is so important, that even if it were to cost physical disability it would be worth it.

You see church we're supposed to be the salt of the Earth, the light of the world. If we don't get it right what chance is there for the rest? Don't you know we're supposed to be the only institution which exists for the benefit of non -members?

BOB? ... I NEVER KNEW YOU WERE A CHRISTIAN

So don't moan, that's our job description. And don't think we've got to go round spouting and door knocking, that only irritates people; much better to use example.
"Preach a sermon every day and if you have to use words" said St Francis of Assisi.

And don't judge! "Don't pick on people, jump on their failures criticize their faults- unless of course you want the same treatment".–(Matt. 7:1. Message)

Because:
"They and only they that are obedient at my coming and they that have fallen asleep being such, shall I gather unto me (in the air) at my coming".

Now we all know the Bible's full of Judgement Day theology. And I know the Looney fringe love to put the wind up the un-initiated with this one to what has amounted to much detriment and church discredit over the years. The idea of cosmic intervention during recent years put ET centre stage and even gave copious amounts of fuel to the UFO devotees. With the advances of science and billions of dollars spent on the search for extra-terrestrial intelligence (e.g. SETI). The intelligentsia of this world and the gurus of academia would have us believe that we are not alone. And who are we to question that when space is so vast that there are supposed to be more stars in the universe than all the grains of sand on earth. "Little green men talk" usually gets good conversation and nodding approval even though it may often carry an air of humour. But the reality of it all is that we are *not* alone. The Bible makes it very plain that the day will come when the Earth shall witness cosmic intervention, but not ET. ET is fantasy, Jesus is reality!

Because:
"Then they'll see the Son of Man enter in grand style, His arrival filling the sky—no one will miss it! He'll dispatch the angels, they will pull in the chosen from the four winds, from pole to pole". (Mark.13:26-27.Message). *"Then we who are alive and remain shall be caught up together with them in the clouds to meet the Lord in the air".*(1Thessalonians.4:17).

How plain is that? The ones who have *not fallen asleep* (in other words died and gone to Heaven already) "shall be changed", transformed and taken away "in the moment in the blink of an eye" No doubt there will be those who will interpret the sudden disappearance of millions as some kind of alien abduction, and I suppose to a God hating world that will be so. But the fact remains that the *Second Coming* of the Messiah is biblical prophecy. It was right about the first time Jesus came 2000 years ago, and it will be right about the second. Make sure you're in the first house, don't get left behind.

Prophecies and predictions have fascinated mankind from time immemorial and their accuracy has often swung from the sublime to the ridiculous. Although reasonable "predictions" can be calculated based on past occurrences, it is sometimes nothing more than wisdom gained through experience; the world stock markets do their best to apply this concept every day. Of course we know there have been some amazingly perceptive people in the past who have offered wise council to leaders and kings; Joseph the interpreter of dreams is such an example. But mumbo jumbo and crossing the odd palm or two with silver, searching for the proverbial "tall dark stranger" with a bag of cash, which has always charmed and tickled the ears of the gullible, is not prophecy. The fact remains that we cannot *know* the future but God can, and not only that - He has given us all the information we need in the Bible about the major events yet to come in the history of the universe. About these events we can have absolute confidence because He is never wrong and never lies. 4 This is biblical prophecy and compared with any other weird concocted drivel it stands in an entirely different league. All the information we *need* to know. Not what we *want* to know or think we can work out using some computerised or mystical gimmick. This is not a new hype about the Middle East based on some TV evangelist's latest prophecy-fashion looking for "bottoms on seats in church". No, when Jesus was

pestered by those wanting to know end time signs He responded with the parable of the fig tree:
When you see the tree bearing fruit you know Summer is near. So in the same way when you see global wars and chaos approaching you know the end is near, in fact at the very door ! (Mark 13).
And that's about as good as it needs to get. And that's about as much as you need to know for now! If that's not plain what is? Jesus was man of common sense as well as Son of God. Your job and mine is to make sure we are ready, always ready *"for the day of the Lord will come like a thief in the night,* (1Thess 5:2.) ---- Don't be caught napping !
Because:
"***Not all that say that they believed I died and rose again will I gather at my coming. But they and they only that believe and live that belief ------.***"

"***For there are many who profess my name, who are linked up with the world. They reject my teaching that I have taught.***
They cannot serve God and Mammon."
(SUCH WILL I NOT GATHER)

"Money, money, money
Must be funny
In the rich man's world"-
- goes the song—

And "funny" (strange) it is !
Money (or mammon being wealth and possessions) is neutral but the love of it is not.
Here's what a few millionaires have had to say about it in the past:

- *I have made millions, but they have brought me no* happiness --- Rockefeller
- *The care of 200,000,000 is enough to kill anyone. There is no pleasure in it* ----Vanderbilt
- *I am the most miserable man on earth* .----- John Jacob Astor.
- *What can I say? I only know I am desolate*.--------- J Paul Getty.
- *I was happier when doing a mechanic's job*.------- Henry Ford.
- *Millionaires seldom smile*.-------Andrew Carnegie.

But then money will buy:

- *A bed but not sleep.*
- *Books but not brains.*
- *Food but not appetite.*
- *Finery but not beauty.*
- *A house but not a home.*
- *Medicine but not health.*
- *Luxuries but not culture.*
- *Amusement but not happiness.*
- *A crucifix but not a Saviour.*
- *Religion but not Salvation*
- *A good life but not eternal life.*
- *A passport to everywhere but Heaven.* **5.**

And don't forget:*" It' easier for a camel to pass through the eye of a needle than for a rich man to enter the kingdom of God."-* (Mark 10:25).

The Bible has over two thousand references to money and possessions and sixteen of Jesus' parables out of His thirty eight deal with the handling of money. In almost every case the message has emphasised the importance of need as opposed to greed. *"If you have two coats, give one away," he said. "Do the same with your food."* (Luke 3:11. *Message*).

We don't have to be too clever to see this false god as not just a violation of the 1st and 2nd commandments but also as a worm which has burrowed its way into almost every part of western culture. Sadly the "prosperity doctrine" has not only crept into society but commands a good set of ears in the church as well. Blame the telly or education if you must but the fact remains that as Christians we do have choices. God will supply all our needs not our wants, is supposed to be the faith. Trendy vicars, gospel divas and churches full of gimmicks, flashing lights and loud decibels are ok as long as God's in charge of the "voltage". When it supersedes the gospel don't forget it's the Holy Spirit who pulls the plug. And sadly many churches seem to operate quite well without God these days - some would rather preach money first. Let's face-it-in a society propped up with good insurance services, pensions and a welfare state who needs to make life difficult?

This kind of faith is easy. – A game !

I'm told that the underground church in the Far East including China is flourishing. Not financially because its members don't have much, but against strong Communist opposition it stands as a spiritual giant, even in spite of some church buildings being bulldozed and a total lack of grants.

I'm told that many of these Christians, live in fear of being arrested and tortured for their faith, and have learned to rely on God for just about everything including not just the next meal but where the next place might be to lay their head.

Yet I read how Yonggi Cho in Korea has the largest church in the world with a congregation of around one million .**6.**

I am also told that according to figures taken in 2003 China is seeing a growth rate of approximately 30,000 new Christians per year and that the "born again" rate could even exceed the birth rate. **7** And by 2030 there could be more church goers in China than USA.

And of course I read in the New Testament how twelve ordinary men preached the gospel to the world because they were fired by witness to the Resurrection of Jesus in the face of magnitudinal opposition.

Have we forgotten what *"Spirit we're* supposed to be *of* ?" Or are we too comfortable to bother ? (Luke 9:55)

You see: " ***There are many who are in connection with my church, that has bitterness within them. That is not my pattern. Such*** *I will not gather."*
"Also, there are such in my church that carries within them an envious spirit. That is not my spirit. Such will I *NOT* ***gather at my coming.***

I again recall the story of Brother Yun, a remarkable Christian in the underground church in China, who was imprisoned and cruelly treated for his faith. This man who had suffered much physical abuse under Chinese authorities, and thought he had probably seen it all, was to find yet another form of persecution when he eventually escaped China in 2001 and came to the West. Until that time any suffering he encountered was helped to be more bearable through his knowing that he was part of a wider loyal and loving Christian community, all of the same mind and supporting one another. But his expectations were to be shattered when he found a totally different attitude amongst some westerners. Many churches he visited were found to be sceptical and antagonistic towards him. Gossiping and backbiting, disbelief and immoral living was something he had not fully experienced amongst his fellow Christians back in

China. This was new, a form of mental persecution which was not so much from outside the church but from within! 8.

Gossiping and backbiting. Sneering and murmuring about the preacher when he's trying to do his best, jockeying for positions of power and control in the church are all poison in the pot and are certainly NOT the Jesus pattern. Yet we see it, do nothing about it and if not careful join it. It grieves the Holy Spirit and it's rotten to the core! This is NOT the Jesus pattern!

It's time for us to stop playing religious games with God. It's time to get serious. it's no longer good enough just to "believe" in Jesus; we need to become His disciples…. 9.

"----there are such that profess and proclaim my name But for their unloyalty of living which is contrary to my pattern which causeth strife and division in my church, such will I not gather."
" For they are unholy!"
No one can deceive me, I know the life of all. There is such in my church that possesses jealousy, hatred and has tongues that are used more for backbiting than for my glory. Yet they profess my name. But they shall be left behind, for they are unholy"

"Saith the Lord"

Don't be naive. There are difficult times ahead.
As the end approaches, people are going to be self-absorbed, money-hungry, self-promoting, stuck-up, profane, contemptuous of parents, crude, coarse, dog-eat-dog, unbending, slanderers, impulsively wild, savage, cynical, treacherous, ruthless, bloated windbags, addicted to lust, and allergic to God.
They'll make a show of religion, but behind the scenes they're animals. Stay clear of these people. (2 Timothy 3:1-5 .The Message.)

I would think that this just about covers the lot! It shouldn't take much imagination to read between the lines here. No need to harp on about drugs, drink, pornography, adultery, incest, rape, murder etc. and every other vile filth which is an abomination to God. The signs are here, the tide's coming in and sandbags at the church door won't keep the sewage out if it's got friends on the inside!

You see. If you twist the truth it'll twist you! Be warned! The Devil has no problem in wearing a crucifix or sitting in a comfortable pew. Compromise is one of his best cards and he can be so PC. - even nice! He loves raising new "messiahs" and "prophets", and if he can't bring you down he'll puff you up. And hey! He even believes in God! In fact he can sell you the latest worship package.

He's not only a craftsman of religion and a good spin doctor, but a high authority on the Bible.

He even has his own version, or rather perversion, of Christianity, including "miracles". Fortune telling, spoon-bending, Reiki, spiritualism, astrology and many more occult practices and counterfeit doctrine are all part of his "attractive" Christian witchcraft package. And I bet somebody you know will probably have one! **10.**

Or he'll probably slip it in under a nice respectable guise drawn from dominant eastern religions hailed by the *power-back-in-the- church* brigade as a "come and benefit from what the multi-faith church can offer" deal, and guaranteeing a low cringe factor on the gospel.

Healing meetings often attract, the sick, desperate, and glory seekers who want to dabble, try their hand at a spot of New Age evening class Reiki and crystal gazing, followed by a nice beneficial massage for good measure.------

And oo! You will feel better!

No! church.

There's no place for cheap imitations and dodgy counterfeits here because

:*"The Holy Spirit should continually fill and overflow you. When this happens, you will start to see miracles and many people coming to salvation, just as in the Bible. I want to share with you the key secret of how Christians can experience a continual flow of living water in their lives. In my opinion, this key is the one major thing. The answer is not to attend more Christian conferences or seek new ministers with new messages. Please listen carefully. The key for experiencing the flow of God's living water in your life is...Obedience."*- Brother Yun. **11.**

So:

My gathering will be my pattern and my pattern only as taught in my Sermon on the Mount.

This is the Jesus pattern:

Tell them Psalm 1 :

Blessed is the one
who does not walk in step with the wicked
or stand in the way that sinners take
or sit in the company of mockers,
but whose delight is in the law of the LORD,
and who meditates on his law day and night.----------------
-------------For the LORD watches over the
way of the righteous,
but the way of the wicked leads to destruction.

Well how does one close such a message as this?

There seems to be very little left to say now, as I like you probably feel helplessly transfixed by the ear shattering silence.

My real concern from the study and preaching of this sermon is that there will be many who will fall short, yet who claimed to be Christian. They even did all the churchy things like prayer meetings, communion, did charitable acts and demonstrated some form of godliness, but who never knew the true love and power of a born-again relationship gained through positive obedience to Jesus. In other words they never had the assurance within that they were saved. (Rom. 8:16-17)

In my somewhat dramatized way of trying to open up the message of Pastor Sanderson as received "whilst in the beyond" all those years ago I realise that such a message can be highly cringy and heavy. But then I don't care. Shoot the messenger, burn the book, mock, moan, groan, blog the internet if you must, but please don't complain when you cock it up at the Star-gate, lest you hear someone echo yonder; "Well I told you so"!

Pastor Sanderson's wake-up call and apparent corrective drive is, I'm sure, meant to have a positive aim and reminds me of the pruning of the vine analogy in John chapter 15. Getting rid of dead wood and clutter in our lives will and can I'm sure bring forth much fruit and is a refining process that can only be beneficial to our lives, provided our motives and intentions are pure and sincere. But that of course takes effort and responsibility on our behalf and complacency will find many an escape route. We know the rewards can be great in that when church decides to become Church she is unstoppable. History proves that, and its beacons of light have been many an encouraging example to follow. Being a part of this kind of universal team is an exciting and unique invitation. An invitation which not only asks us to help make a difference to this shabby world we have helped create but to discover our true identity, realise our full potential, and become the best that we can be.

And here endeth the lesson --- **Amen**

Summary

Well we've had the good ol' fashioned hell fire sermon, which was probably more of a Divine riot act than a nice three point landing. We've had the strong medicine and the spoon of jam at the end to help it go down. Unfortunately there weren't many sugar coated pills, but then I don't suppose there would be many of those around either in the early 1900s when this sermon was first preached. So to be fair why should we be treated any differently? Furthermore one might add that if the church and the world need sorting out then they're going to have to take some strong medicine anyway, sooner or later. This of course is the main drive of William's message and is vital to this book before considering science and philosophy. On the other hand perhaps we are meant to take this as encouragement, meaning that a strong lesson of discipline can lead to correction, as the Bible puts it:

"He who heeds discipline shows the way to life, but whoever ignores correction leads others astray." (Proverbs 10:17).

This can only take us to an all important position -- repentance!

The past has shown that before the world can be put right the church has to get a shaking first, otherwise its message is powerless. Brother Yun's story as told in his book "*The Heavenly Man*" is a very good example of what a 21st century supernatural church is capable of under persecution with the right mind set. When the church is in this kind of fit shape anything is possible, even raising the dead! For us in the West however our intellectualism and way of life can grossly hinder faith. "We would rather debate a question without settling it than settle a question without debating it". putting faith low down on the priority list. **12** But if debate and criticism causes one to be true to one's own self I can only surmise that in time such honesty and self-awareness will reveal within us our frailties and shortcomings, and in this respect it would probably be a good thing. The Bible tells us that "all have fallen short of the glory of God" (Rom.3:23) and none of us is good enough or capable by our own efforts to enter Heaven. We have all been tainted and marred by what the Bible calls "original sin" caused by man's disobedience in the Garden of Eden, and whether we like it or not it is a corruption which is now part of our DNA. The church therefore cannot afford to sit comfortably thinking that being "saved" implies it has arrived, when in reality its saints can never be truly "saved" until they arrive in Heaven, and must constantly "stay awake" as Jesus advised. (Mark 13:33-37)

The church is not the only one who needs to respond to this message. This message is for everyone else who does not know Jesus as personal Saviour and Lord. Because we cannot get to Heaven on our own merit, we need to repent of our sins, (ask God to forgive our mistakes, misdeeds and failures of the past), then invite Jesus to come in to our life and allow His Holy Spirit to clean us up and make us fit for Heaven. It is He who saves us and sets us free from the law of sin and death. It is He who enables us to be born again and so to access a new plan for our lives. It is He who re-tunes us to the frequency of the kingdom of Heaven and it is He who makes us good enough, and that starts with repentance.

"For by Grace we are saved through faith. And this is not from yourselves, it is the gift of God". (Eph.2:8).

Conclusion

The message given by Jesus "whilst in the beyond" was transcribed by Pastor William Sanderson and formatted for use as his personal sermon notes.

Although the message was meant to be a wake-up call for the church of his day it can readily be applied to the church of our day.

That the world needs a Saviour; has been given a Saviour and needs to personally receive that Saviour is a commonly understood biblical message.

The extension of this message therefore has to apply to the whole of mankind and not just the church.

Notes and References.

1. W E H Leckey. Historian; 1838 – 1903.States:"if it had not been for Wesley and his followers, tumbrels might have carried victims to the guillotine in an English revolution like the French Revolution."Cited:

New Interest in John Wesley; Francis J. McConnell , *The journal of Religion.* (University of Chicago Press: Oct., 1940 Vol. 20, No.4), p. 340

2. A. G. Gardiner. Born, Alfred George Gardiner 1865. Chelmsford, Essex, England. Died, 1946. Occupation, Journalist, editor, and author.
Campaign against certain social injustices particularly working conditions in industry.

3 Mother Teresa Quotes. Ref: About.com quotations. 2013

4. Wayne Grudem. *Systematic Theology*, (Leicester: Intervarsity Press. 2005). P. 1091

5 Robert J. Morgan. "Preacher's Sourcebook", (Nashville: Nelson publishing). Ref.575.

6 Yonggy Cho. David Yonggi Cho (formerly known as Paul Yonggi Cho) is a Korean Christian minister. He is Senior Pastor and founder of the Yoido Full Gospel Church (Assemblies of God), the world's largest congregation with a membership of 1,000,000 (as of 2007). Cho still conducts two services of the seven the church holds a

day; they are so heavily attended that people often must arrive an hour early to have a seat. Ref. Wikkipedia. 2013

7 Paul Hattaway. "Back to Jerusalem", (Milton Keynes: Authentic Books.

8 Brother Yun. http://johnharmstrong.typepad.com/john_h_armstrong_/2008/09/smoke-and-fire.html Paul Hattaway comments on some of the attitudes found in some Western churches.

9 Brother Yun. *Living Water.* Zondervan. 2008. (Quote cited: *irememberthepoor.org/.../**brother-yun**-insight-into-the-western-**church***)

10 Craig S. Hawkins. "Witchcraft. Exploring the World of Wicca". Baker Books. Grand Rapids. 1996.

11 Brother Yun. *Living Water.* Zondervan. 2008.

12 Quote from *Pensées* (Thoughts) of Joseph Joubert. 7thMay 1754 – 4thMay 1824. A French essayist and moralist whose work was published posthumously.

Facing the Star-gate

Chapter 10.

Grace - the Final Frontier !

The phrase: "To boldly go where no man has ever gone before" was repeatedly quoted at the beginning of just about every "Star Trek" TV series. So much so that it easily became adopted into every day chit-chat and banter; that is of course amongst the initiated. However corny it might sound it is indeed true that throughout the millennia Man's quest has always seemed to be to explore and push the boundaries. The infinity of space is not only fascinating but mysterious. One cannot, dare not, help feeling that sense of awe and wonder when gazing at the heavens on a clear un-polluted starry night. Imagine being in a boat floating on a sleeping smooth moonlit ocean, gazing at a vast universe only to realise that you are probably suspended between two of the greatest forces in eternity, the heavens above and the waters below !

Now if that doesn't conjure up God thoughts maybe the fear of an on-coming storm and risk of drowning just might!

Ideas of infinity and eternity are as much philosophical as they are scientific. I have tried to point this out in some of my previous chapters. I have also tried to establish the importance of the spiritual dimension in all this which I feel is an inevitable path for us all. In this final chapter I hope to show how grace is the ultimate state that humanity can ever hope to achieve whilst on this planet, and probably the most difficult mountain to climb. We cannot ponder and debate the science of origins for very long without bringing God into it sooner or later. The foolish thing to do is to leave Him out. This only limits us in our quest for knowledge and in turn renders a disservice to mankind as a whole.

So to "boldly go" by taking a step of faith also means we might boldly have to face some kind of opposition. In fact it's unavoidable. Little Jacob, in ch.6, refused to be intimidated by his teacher and David faced Goliath. Christianity is not a soft option. The trouble is some Christians have gone soft, thinking that grace is all about Easter bunnies, Santa Clause and just being nice.

Mark Twain once said: "Some people are good in the worst sense of the word". **1**

A sacrifice of grace

The picture I get of the New Testament is nothing like that. When Jesus was around he pushed the boundaries and ran the risk. There was no one more controversial, radical or advanced for his time than Jesus. Opponent of religiosity, academic pomposity and finger-pointing, hypocritical dogma, Jesus demonstrated a new way which superseded any religious, philosophical or political ideology of the day. Although the religious observances and laws were good, if applied correctly, for a healthy moral society and family life, Jesus demonstrated the heart of the Law, fulfilled its purpose and showed its relevance. In other words He made it connect. Such a manifestation has to shake the foundations. And shake them it did! But notice His style. He didn't do it by force, fierce debate or any other contrivance of man but by the simple power of grace. Like little Jacob He simply said it as it was: boldly, humbly and in the power of truth. This is grace, the Jesus pattern. And notice the reaction. The child's teacher also showed grace in her honest response. Grace is infectious. Following this path is following Jesus and I believe is the highest level of civilization one can attain both in this world and the next. Ironically of course Jesus made enemies as well as friends, and this was the price because ultimately grace may require some sacrifice. Grace is not popular amongst evil men because in a fallen world like ours force apparently gets the results and is proven to work. Force is the mainspring of *the survival of the fittest.* Grace is also un-popular for another reason. It is because its enemies cannot comprehend the way every act of violence towards it draws a response of unconditional love and for many a type that's too much to handle, because "the gates of hell cannot prevail against it". (Matt.Ch.16:18).

So what exactly is this Grace?

A simple definition would be: "Unmerited favour from God". A more down to earth example might be like a traffic warden who has to give you a ticket because you've broken the law but then goes on to pay the fine himself. -

- I know, that would be a miracle!

Another illustration might be the one about two donkeys on a narrow single track mountain path, heading towards each other. On one side there is a steep cliff face on the other a sheer drop of several hundred feet. They both glare at each other as they advance head to head in fierce determination. Having already made up their mind not to give way, it seems an obvious deadlock, and impossible for them both to pass without one ending up in the deep ravine. After several minutes of agonising stubbornness one simply lies down on his belly and allows the other to climb over the top of him; both peacefully and happily go on their way.

There's no problem in finding a good definition of grace with a nice rounded example to drive the idea home. But I think a wise move would be to draw an example from someone who has more experience and who is better at illustration. Philip Yancey's *What's so amazing about Grace* does such a splendid job and is well worth a read:

American Yancey grew up in the Deep South. Although committed Baptist he admits that he was unavoidably a racist. The legal system of apartheid drew a firm wedge between blacks and whites to the extent that blacks were cruelly persecuted. He recalls how the noble Martin Luther King bravely challenged the regime of hatred by developing a sophisticated strategy for war fought with grace not gunpowder. Apparently he never refused to meet with his adversaries. He opposed policies but not personalities. But most importantly he encountered violence with non-violence, and hatred with love. "let us not seek to satisfy our thirst for freedom by drinking from the cup of bitterness and hatred," he exhorted his followers. "We must not allow our creative protest to degenerate into physical violence. Again and again we must rise to the majestic heights of meeting physical force with soul force." King said "We must awaken a sense of shame in the oppressor and challenge his sense of superiority. ----The end is reconciliation; the end is redemption; the end is the creation of the beloved community." Yancey goes on to say how the grace that King finally set in motion disarmed his own stubborn evil. **2**

Martin Luther King's methods were not unique. He had studied how Mahatma Ghandi used similar ideas in tackling a cruel British regime in India. Gandhi called it "satyagraha" – A form of passive resistance which could be summed up as the force of peace, truth and love.

When Gandhi was asked how such methods would have worked in Nazi controlled Germany he had this to say:

"If I were a Jew and were born in Germany and earned my livelihood there, I would claim Germany as my home even as the tallest Gentile German might, and challenge him to shoot me or cast me in the dungeon; I would refuse to be expelled or to submit to discriminating treatment. And for doing this I should not wait for the fellow Jews to join me in civil resistance, but would have confidence that in the end the rest were bound to follow my example. If one Jew or all the Jews were to accept the prescription here offered, he or they cannot be worse off than now. And suffering voluntarily undergone will bring them an inner strength and joy." **3**

Ultimately one cannot find a more powerful example than that of Christ's atoning death on the cross

On a recent visit to Israel I was quite disturbed to hear a Jewish local historian comment: "where was God in the Holocaust?" whilst giving us his theological views as a liberal Jew. I had to admit that for a few minutes I was silenced in thought and word, and I suppose one could say that there's no answer to that. After all if God had withdrawn because of man's fall at Eden did that mean He was no longer around to care? We were heading towards Golgotha at the time and whether or not it was because I was pre-occupied with the visit to the site of the crucifixion I don't know, but suddenly the thought stuck me with yet an even bigger question - where was God at the crucifixion? The scriptures tell us He was absent! "My God my God why have you abandoned me?" went the cry from Jesus. (Matt.27:45-46). And so the thought that followed was this: Could it just be that God was absent from the horror of looking at the cross because, in essence, He was Himself nailed to it? And man has been "nailing" him to it ever since? So where was God in the Holocaust? Could it be He was in the gas chamber, suffering yet again along with the victims of cruelty? Even in our so called civilized world Hitler's words like "The final solution to the Jewish problem" are terrible echoes of a form of anti-Christian social Darwinism which seems to be an in-bred latent force within the very fabric of humanity and if anything only show us up for what we are. When God incarnate suffered to the point of death on the cross the force of evil was allowed to do its worst. But God demonstrated a far greater force; that of love against which the devil had no power, and the resurrection which surpasses any invention of the human mind, changed the course of history and re-opened the new *star-gate*. –"O death where is thy sting? O grave where is thy victory?" (1Cor.15:55.) AV

God, in His grace sent Jesus Christ to take our place. Every punishment and curse that should come upon us because of our sin, he has taken upon himself so that instead of judgement we may receive blessings.

Isaiah prophesied about the grace of Jesus Christ perfectly:-

"Surely He has borne our griefs. And carried our sorrows;

Yet we esteemed Him stricken. Smitten by God, and afflicted.

But He was wounded for our transgressions, He was bruised for our iniquities; the chastisement for our peace was upon Him. And by His stripes we are healed." (Isa.53:4-5).

In the end it's not laws which change people's lives but grace.

Religion.

Sadly there's a great deal of un-grace that can worm itself into Christianity. I've often heard it said that the worst thing that happened to Christianity was religion. Even Richard Dawkins would probably have to agree with that one. We must not forget that it was the religious system of the day which crucified Christ and things such as rules, dogma and laws are as much a part of every-day life as eating and breathing. We love it! As soon as some new good idea arrives it has to have a new rule book to go with it. The trouble is the rule book can finish up having more clout than the "new idea". And so it may seem to be the case sometimes with Christianity. The Gospel of God's Grace was, and is, simple – "Love God and love your neighbour as yourself" (not forgetting enemies), and that's just about it, because if sincere, then the Holy Spirit will do the rest of the work within us and for us, "and you need not for any man to teach you- *these inner spiritual truths*."-(1 John 2:27), *my emphasis*. Unfortunately because we are human we often slip into the mould of having to find ways to handle or control "things" so we construct special "handles" as it were, or in the case of religion, rituals in order to help us get the "thing" right. These very "handles" which were once designed to be language guidance to help operate our devotions etc. should be helpful, (in fact ritual and traditions can become important living markers along life's road and a tremendous aid to worship) but when religion becomes centre stage God can finish up in the audience, or maybe not in the theatre at all! And that is a recipe for disaster. At this point the tail wags the dog, religion becomes an irrelevant empty shell and another man made system or ideology. P.C. politics, science, sport, art etc, all have their little tin gods of control and power. And on this note I can almost agree with Dawkins when he says:

"We are all atheists about most of the gods that humanity has ever *believed* in. Some of us go one god further". **4**

Although I might swap the word *believed* for *invented.*

So who's right ?

C S Lewis.

There's a famous story about C S Lewis which I think is a tremendous key to all this:

During a British conference on comparative religions, experts from around the world were discussing whether any one belief was unique to the Christian faith. They began eliminating possibilities. Incarnation? Other religions had different versions of gods appearing in human form. Resurrection? Again, other religions had accounts of return from death. The debate went on for some time, until C. S. Lewis wandered into the room. "What's the rumpus about?" he asked, and heard in reply that his colleagues were discussing Christianity's unique contribution among world religions. In his forthright manner, Lewis responded, "Oh, that's easy. It's grace."(Rom. 5:20). Where sin abounds grace abounds much more. **5**

The Greeks sought for the "Logos" and philosophised upon it. Hawking searched for the theory of everything and made a science of it. The Jews had the Ten Commandments and structured it. Islam tried to do better, imposed more laws and enforced it. And some Christians so feared the road to hell, that in their failure to enjoy the path to Heaven, they made a heavy religion out of it.

So this is how I see it: The Biblical worldview is that every culture and belief system once had their origins in the same pre-Judaic, post-flood roots according to the description of the spreading out of nations in the book of Genesis. If so one might expect that there could be something of a remnant and a common thread, within the heart of many such cultures; a kind of "latent nostalgic Eden" or just simply the search for happiness and fulfilment. Of course grace sometimes appears in religions other than Christianity. Bruce Nicholls, in his *AFFIRM* booklet *Is Jesus the Only Way to God?*, writes:

"Glimpses of grace are found in every religion for there is an awareness among all people of the majesty of God, the Creator (Romans 1:20) and of the law of conscience (Romans 2:14-15). In moments of true self-knowledge men and women despair of finding God by their own effort and cry out to God for mercy. This awareness of shame and guilt is itself evidence that the living God through the Holy Spirit is at work in every human heart calling them back to God. It is a sign of grace." **6.**

Unfortunately many belief systems have collected so much baggage and myth that any biblical resemblance may have become so distorted, almost to a point beyond recognition, that in order to pan for any "gold" one would have to shift a huge pile of man-made clutter. What makes Christianity unique is that its gospel, in fulfilment through Jesus, sprang out of a living Jewish faith which had the hallmark of God's hand on it from the very beginning, notwithstanding of course any baggage that Judaism had collected prior to Jesus and any that Christianity has collected since. But when we distil away all this dross, I think perhaps like C S Lewis, we can come to a very simple conclusion:

Any of the great world religions whose objective is humanity as well as the Divine cannot be far off the mark. As Jesus might say "they are not far from the Kingdom of God" – this was pointed out in the story in Mark's Gospel chapter 12 verse 34. However the pious man in the story, who came to Jesus with questions, kept all the rules and was certainly on the right track, yet despite his devout belief he was still in-complete. Comparing this with a mathematical illustration it's almost like saying that many positive belief systems have within their equations several quantities of truth. But that's about as far as it can go until the unknown quantities in the equation are known. Hawking was probably treading a similar path with his search for the theory of everything. Jesus however, is not so much the equation but the answer! And this is why the Bible strongly emphasises that "Salvation is found in no-one else, for there is no other name under heaven given to men by which we must be saved" (Acts.4:12. NIV). Perhaps this is what C S Lewis may have had in mind when he made his sweeping comment about "grace" because Jesus is the ultimate fulfilment of that *Grace* ! Religion or philosophy may take us a long way in the right direction but ultimately will be found to fall short; otherwise there is no purpose in Christ's sacrificial death on the cross, which was for our benefit and salvation. God's grace is the gift of Jesus to mankind which is meant to be received through the singularity of faith. This is the Word incarnate –Heaven being earthed – the *Logos.* The religious structure or cultural environment is secondary.

There's a very famous story in chapter 18 of Acts of the Apostles in the New Testament where St. Paul points out to the Greeks that there is an unknown god within their belief pantheon of many gods. He goes on to identify this as the Creator who must be recognised if their understanding is to be complete.

Similarly in recent times there have been some remarkable accounts of whole Hindu, Buddhist and Muslim communities accepting Jesus as Lord but still retaining their cultural/religious routines. Missionary societies such as YWAM (Youth With a Mission) who preach "keep your own religion, just add Jesus" claim witness to this kind of experience. However such transformations are not straight forward .

What has sometimes been interpreted as a westernized approach has unfortunately alienated them from their friends and family to such an extent that they have been violently rejected from their community.

Also strong pagan beliefs have sometimes diluted the gospel of grace into nothing more than a distorted version of Christianity. 7 However the fact remains that because the gospel of God's grace has power to transcend religion full stop, we must not throw the "baby out with the bath-water". Instead we must not *"copy the behaviour and customs of the world but let God transform you into a new person by changing the way you think. Then you will know what God wants you to do and you will know how good and pleasing and perfect His will is."* (Rom.12:2) New Living Translation.

So there we have it, no matter what a person's cultural background is, there is always a place for Jesus at the table.

Grace the ultimate authority

When the Creator placed into Man's DNA latent defence mechanisms for survival He also had a Master plan for Man's ultimate destiny and salvation. Against what would appear to be a backdrop of darkness, doom and selfish wickedness throughout history, beacons of light have appeared with increasing brilliance as the darkness thickened. Reflected in the initial act of Creation when God commanded light to appear into a world of chaos and darkness this parallel seems to have been personified in many of the remarkable acts of compassion and grace we humans are capable of in spite of all our shortcomings. And what better beacon was God's Son

himself, Jesus, "Word which became flesh ---- the Light of men, living amongst us in the power of Grace and Truth" (John:1). This was not some new tin-pot politician or warmonger or scientist. If God thought the world needed to send one of those Jesus would have been one of those. But because the world needed rescuing from a lost eternity He sent a Saviour. Remember; "we are not dealing with flesh and blood but principalities and powers and the spiritual rulers of this dark world" (Eph.6). The conflict is not so much in the seen world but in the unseen. The battle is between the forces of good and evil and if we can't see that in the unseen world at least let's have no excuse for not seeing it in the seen world. Switch the television on, the news is full of it!
When God sent His Son to planet Earth He knew the message would cost Jesus his life. Jesus, Son of Man, friend of sinners and the downtrodden who healed the sick, cured the lame, made the blind see and even raised the dead, was finally to engage the full force of evil.
"The stage had been set for the greatest drama in history during which man would do his worst and God would give His best." **8**

The crucifixion was grotesque but the Resurrection glorious! The devil had played the ace card – death, and failed! Christ is Risen! Satan's power and authority is broken and re-taken. Jesus has conquered hell and death. Risen conquering Son, who did it through the power of grace! God through His Son and Saviour Jesus Christ had pierced the satanic darkness of this world and created a new *star-gate* to Heaven - the "New Eden" - "where the lion will once more lie down with the lamb" -

- a place beyond the stars now connecting Earth with a Highway for God's new people, "and a child shall lead them"! (Isaiah11:6).

God's plan was and still is paradise. A perfect world of beauty, love, peace and harmony; man and God, hand in hand forever. Yet because we're all on a journey and at a point of time in eternity, the story is still to unfold. We know that this life is definitely not all that there is and we also know that *the whole of creation awaits for the redemption* (Rom.8:19-23). We can rest assured that "Thy will be done on earth as it is in Heaven" is a certainty, despite some cocky little upstart (the devil) fouling the works. God is a master at turning disaster into success, which means that the struggles and misfortunes we now experience are all within His permissive will and purpose. This does not make God into a cruel and uncaring sadist as some in their short sightedness try to suggest, but rather the opposite. To say why can't God just come down and seize control, get rid of all the bad guys and make us good would mean He would have to remove our freedom of choice and God-given freewill, which would make us like robots and take away our individual responsibility. God is love and He has created a world where love is possible. And that love can only operate within the freedom He has given.

The question of Christ's crucifixion and suffering in general follows little earthly logic, yet we cannot dispute the existence of an all-powerful God and his son Jesus, (1Cor.1:21). Neither can we ignore the powerful evidence for the Bible's accuracy for the origin of civilisation and the Garden of Eden. When we consider all the evidence and many explanations from world religions and philosophy the biblical worldview is the only one that fits every time, but it only operates through the dimension of a living faith and that was the reason I needed to share my thoughts and produce this book. Once the thin veil between belief and non-belief is penetrated the light flows in and understanding takes place. For we "draw nigh to God that he might draw nigh to us" (James.4:8),

In other words we don't understand that we might believe, but believe that we might understand. At this point of faith the spark jumps, salvation happens, and the Pentecostal flame is lit!

And so to end.

We've heard a powerful story about a man called William Sanderson and I'd like to think his testimony and message has been a catalyst to challenge, stir-up and provoke discussion and debate among believers and non-believers alike. I have also aired some of the theories and ideas postulated by some of the world's science gurus, particularly those who subscribe to a party-line worldview. As a result I hope that the reader can be more discerning in what he or she is exposed to via the media, as trickery and corruption exist at all levels. (I must also include religion in this which needn't think that it can get off the hook either). I'd also like to think that I have exposed the belief of non-belief as being a faith within itself, because I am convinced that people who claim to believe in nothing will believe in anything, which sadly makes them the most gullible. There will of course be those who will doubt, criticize and jeer anyway. I'm expecting that. Hopefully there will be those who will praise and even cheer - that's good news! But the ones

that might concern me most are the ones who are just left cold, without spirit. They are the ones whom I believe are the furthest to reach.
This book was intended to encourage those who were on the road and also to open up the way to others who might see good sense in what I have written and make their own decision to follow Jesus. Remember being a Christian is not a soft option; neither does it make false claims that all will be rosy.
It requires commitment and loyalty to the Master. But the benefits are countless. He promises to be with you. He promises to supply your needs, to heal, to restore, to give fulfilment, peace and joy in the knowledge that your sins are forgiven –past, present and future. But most of all He promises to save you. No other religion or philosophy can claim this guarantee, and that's the difference. Just to think, "maybe I'll have a place in Heaven" isn't an option. Eternity's too dangerous a place to take risks. I want assurance. I want to *know* I'm saved and going to Heaven. This is what the gospel of Jesus is all about - and I say again: no other system on earth can promise that kind of guarantee. Only Jesus can. It is a gift that's already been given but must be sincerely accepted. In the Bible stories, Jesus came where He was invited, and that hasn't changed – so ask Him, invite him in! "Jesus is the same yesterday, today and forever". (Heb.13:8). The new Eden exists, not just as a place beyond the stars but also as a state of heart, through which runs God's highway. We access it by faith and allow His grace to shape and re-tune that new person within. It will take the rest of our life to complete, but then God promises His Holy Spirit will get us there once we have made that commitment. Even now at this very moment, Jesus stands before us; "the way the truth and the life"– The *Star-gate!*

"Amazing Grace how sweet the sound that saved a wretch like me. I once was lost but now I'm found. Was blind but now I see".

John Newton. 1779.

Notes and References.

1. Cited in John Burke: *No perfect people allowed* (Grand Rapids:Zondervan,2005)

2. Philip Yancey. *What's so amazing about Grace.* (Grand Rapids: Zondervan,1997) pp. 130 – 133.

3. Gandhi's comment on the Holocaust http://en.wikipedia.org/wiki/Satyagraha. 04/07/2013

4. Richard Dawkins, *The Root of All Evil* , UK Channel 4, 2006

5. CS Lewis quote in *Exploring Christianity* http://www.christianity.co.nz/grace-13.htm 04/07/2013

6. Bruce Nicholls. Affirm Publications, distributed by Castle Publishing. ISBN: 0958368244

7. Lighthouse Trails Research Project. http://www.lighthousetrailsresearch.com/newmissiology.htm 2013

8. Wiersbe ,Warren W *The Bible Exposition Commentary* (Illinois: Victor Books. Vol 1, 1989), p338.

"Listen to this secret truth: we shall not all die, but when the last trumpet sounds, we shall all be changed in an instant, as quickly as the blinking of an eye.---- "

St. Paul. 1Corinthians ch.15 v 15.

Bibliography

Ashton, Dr. John, "Evolution Impossible" — Master Books, 2012, Green Forest, AR.

Blaiklock, E.M, *The Practice of the Presence of God,* (London: Hodder & Stoughton. 1981).

Blake. William, *The Tiger,* – "Oxford Book of English Verse: 1250 – 1900"

Burke, John, *No perfect people allowed,* (Grand Rapids:Zondervan,2005)

Cooper, Bill, *The Authenticity of the Book of Genesis*, (Portsmouth: Creation Science Movement.2011)

Cooper, Bill, *After the Flood,* (Chichester: New Wine Press, 1995).

Cuozzo Jack "Buried Alive" – the untold story about Neanderthal Man –. 2008, Master Books, Green Forest.

Darwin, Charles, *Origin of Species,* (London: Wordsworth Editions, 1998),

Darwin, Charles, *The Descent of Man,* [London: Penguin Group Publishers. (Plume Book Science, 2007)

Dawkins, Richard, *The God Delusion*, (London: Transworld Publications, 2006).

Dempski, William, *The Delusion of Evolution* (Nottingham: New Life publishing.2010) 4th edition.

Flew, Antony, *There is a God,* (New York, Harper, 2007).

Geisler & Boccino, *Unshakable Foundations*, (Grand Rapids: Bethany House publications, 2001).

Gitt, Werner, *In the Beginning Was Information*, (Stuttgart: CLV Publications. 2000).

Grudem, Wayne, *Systematic Theology*, (Leicester: Intervarsity Press, 2005).

Ham, Ken, *Why won't they listen*, (Green Forest, USA : Master Books.2005).

Hartnett, John, *Starlight Time and the New Physics* (Powder Springs: Creation Book Publishers. 2007).

Hattaway, Paul, *Back to Jerusalem* , (Milton Keynes: Authentic Books, 2003).

Hawking, Stephen, *A Brief History of Time* (London: Bantam Books. 1988).

Hawking, Stephen, *The Grand Design* (London: Bantam Books . 2010),

Hawkins, Craig S, *Witchcraft. Exploring the World of Wicca*, (Grand Rapids: Baker Books. 1996).

Hitler, Adolf, *Mein Kampf,* (Delhi: Jaico Publishing House. 2012)

Jones. Richard G, *God of concrete God of steel* Words copyright 1969 by Galliard Ltd.

Lennox, John, *God and Stephen Hawking* (Oxford: Lion Books. 2010).

Mazur Susan *The Altenburg 16; Expose` of the Evolution Industry*, (Berkley California, North Atlantic Books, 2010).

McIntosh, Andy, *Genesis for Today* (Leominster: Day One Publications. 2001).

Morris, Henry, *New Defender's Bible,* (Nashville: World Publishing, 2006).

Morris, Henry, *The Genesis Record* (Grand Rapids: Baker Publishing, 2007).

Nicholls. Bruce, Affirm Publications, distributed by Castle Publishing. ISBN: 0958368244

Petit, Ian, *The God Who Speaks*, (London: Daybreak Publications, 1989)

Rohl. David, *Legend. The Genesis of Civilization.* (London: Random House (Century Press. 1998).

Ryan & Pitman . *Noah's Flood.* (New York: Simon & Shuster. 1998).

Sarfati, Jonathan, *The Greatest Hoax on Earth,* (Powder Springs: Creation Book Publishers, 2010).

Sarfati Jonathan. *Refuting Compromise* .2004. Master Books, Green Forest.

The Delusion of Evolution. New Life publications 4th edition. 2011.

White. Monty , *What about origins ?* (Leominster: Day One publications. 2010)

Wiersbe, Warren W, *The Bible Exposition Commentary* (Illinois: Victor Books. Vol 1, 1989),

Wilson. Julian , *Wigglesworth the complete story,* (Milton Keynes: Authentic Publishing,2002)

Yancey. Philip, *What's so amazing about Grace*. (Grand Rapids: Zondervan,1997)

Afterword

'Facing the Star-gate'
Exploring the dimension of Faith

This book contains a series of discussion papers to prompt debate, further reading and inspire research on the theme of science and religion or as Rex Brassington states, 'More accurately, science and the Bible'. From the outset science and technology are 'embraced as tools which are a 'means to discover the Creator's handiwork' and also ones which 'might empower the faithful to witness.'

Whilst being thought provoking and challenging this book is also easy to read. One is also aware of the personal nature of the spiritual influences that have had an impact on the writer. Central to the book is the testimony of Pastor William E. Sanderson, which provided Rex with a 'wake-up call and apparent corrective drive' and a reminder to us, especially me, to 'get rid of the dead wood and clutter of our lives' and try to make 'a positive difference in this shabby world we have helped to create, and 'become the best that we can be.'

Looking through the shrouded portal of the Star-gate I tried to catch a glimpse of the sublime. I appreciated Rex's holistic approach, especially his inspirational introduction of poetry alongside the scientific models. I particularly enjoyed Chapter 8 'Patterns---and Blackberries'.

Elizabeth Barrett Browning certainly shows us a glimpse of the 'perfect cosmos' in the quote from her epic poem 'Aurora Leigh', where we see God's presence everywhere as 'Earth's crammed with Heaven'. Stephen Hawking has shared his view on the 'Grand Design' in a magnificent volume, Elizabeth later describes it in seven words when she writes, 'All points coupling with the spinning stars'.

In this work, Rex attempts to integrate science and the Bible and encourage informed dialogue. This exploration of the 'dimension of faith' is to be welcomed, especially if undertaken in gentleness and respect according to guidance from 1 Peter 3:16 and from Philippians 2, where Paul reminds us that Christ's role is based on his humility. Whatever may be the strengths and importance of Christianity, they should arise from that profound sense of humility.

Sometimes when we consider 'the Truth' we mean only 'my truth' and too easily 'God's Will' becomes identified with our own selfish human will; religion often becoming a vehicle for systems of control and abuse in all its forms. This is quite contrary to Jesus' teaching. In this time of awareness of the diversity, unity and equal value of Humankind we remember the Humanity of Christ, which is only different in quality, not in kind. Jesus never sought to make others like Himself. He tried to stimulate them to follow him, to find their own honest response to God who is in them and in all things.

Moreover, as Rex points out, and I believe too, that Jesus was there with the victims of the Holocaust in the Second

World War and with all the Fallen in the trenches and battles of the 'Great War', that we commemorate over the next five years, together with all victims throughout history and sadly, those suffering today and in the future.

A narrow, exclusivist view of Christianity can pose an acute problem in relation to those who have not had the chance to hear the 'Good News' of the gospel of Christ and to respond to it. Can a loving God penalise them for that when it is not their fault? If Christ is the only one who can reveal God to us, why has God allowed human history to develop in a way that limits the number who have access to this? The reality is that other religions have their 'salvation histories' in which God participates.

It was refreshing to read that Rex had included Bruce Nicholls' 'Affirm' booklet, which raises the question: 'Is Jesus the Only Way to God?' We also find those strange bedfellows: CS Lewis, Hawking, Martin Luther King, and St Paul considering aspects of peace, truth, love and grace. Moreover, as Rex points out, 'Any of the great world religions whose objective is humanity as well as the Divine cannot be far off the mark and further that Jesus might say 'are not far from the Kingdom of Heaven.'

As Christians we are often blinkered to these realities. As Rex states, 'Sadly there's a great deal of un-grace that can worm its way into Christianity'. Yet, as he later points out with the help of Jesus and God's amazing Grace and the Holy Spirit, we will reach and pass through the star-gate and see God.' Rex, however, believes that for him it is only through the dimension of his living Christian faith that he 'will draw nigh to God that he might draw nigh to us'.

God is always an infinite mystery beyond our understanding, beyond the scope of our language, symbols, imagery and models of the Divine. These in fact may become a barrier to our spiritual development as they have now become meaningless to many people today. All religious language and symbols are human creations, pointing us to God's 'mysterious doings in all people and all things' including all aspects of science and technology, where we may rediscover God at work within ourselves and in our world, and in partnership with Rex and Elizabeth Browning see 'God's presence and hear the strong clamour of a vehement soul'.

Brenda Pegge BA. PGCE

Former Head Teacher and Education Advisor for Sheffield LEA. Also served as Social Responsibility Officer for Derby Diocese.

34467002R00119

Made in the USA
Charleston, SC
10 October 2014